This is a great new book from my friend, Merrily. This will help all of us follow Jesus more closely. I love her heart for discipleship and equipping the body of Christ.

Brady Boyd, Senior Pastor,
New Life Church, Colorado Springs, Colorado

Merrily Madero has an easily recognizable love and zeal for God. And she possesses that exact same "heart" for God's people! In this book, she deals forthrightly with the principles of "sowing and reaping" using Scriptural examples again and again. She directs followers of Jesus to take genuine responsibility for every area of their lives and points them to true repentance, freedom, and integrity.

Jeff Hlavin, Superintendent,
Assemblies of God Michigan District

Merrily has written a book containing rich wisdom for the Christian walk. Her use of biblical stories while interweaving her own experiences creates a book which is both grounded in Scripture and relevant for the world today. I especially appreciate the questions for reflection at the end of each chapter which allow the reader to immediately personalize lessons learnt. This book is an honest yet sensitive treatment of a challenging topic which I believe will be a significant blessing to many.

Rev Dr Dennis Lum, President, TCA College, Singapore

Do you want freedom from bondage and slavery? Merrily gives practical answers to the difficult questions of how and why. She leaves no doubt about the facts of regretful—and good—choices. And she makes a clear-cut case for abundant, peace-filled living. This gifted woman offers us a catalyst that brings clarity to our vision for an empowered life destiny. Every counselor, pastor, and leader needs this book in their life and library.

Rev. Dr. Lana Heightley, Founder and President of
Women With A Mission, Colorado Springs, Colorado

I have known the author of this book, Merrily Madero, for many years, and she lives what she wrote about in her wonderful book *The Truth About Consequences*. As an officer in our Air Force and as an ordained minister, she has set such a positive example of what it is to be a servant leader who helps others all over the world. Read this book, and it will make a major difference in your day-to-day life.

General Stephen R. Lorenz, USAF, Retired

WHAT IS TRUTH?

My gracious and kind friend and co-partner in ministry with Christ for God's people, Merrily Madero, presents us in her inspiring spiritual reflection *The Truth About Consequences*, a pastoral, personal approach and gospel guidance to deal with those failures, immoral acts, that we call sin and go against the loving will of our kind heavenly Father, and to find God's mercy and forgiveness.

At the heart of Merrily's wise and Scripture-filled book is truth, which she addresses in the first chapter where she explains, what is truth? She weaves this fundamental Christian virtue through all the chapters of her book. Truth or truthfulness is the virtue that consists in showing oneself true in deeds and words and in guarding against duplicity and hypocrisy. Sin comes from the father of all lies, Satan. Every sin is an offense against reason, truth, and right conscience, against the eternal law of God, and brings its own evil consequences and effects. Sin is a failure in genuine love for God and neighbor caused by a perverse attachment to one's own will. It is disobedience against God, and one's desire to become "like gods."

Going through biblical history, Merrily points out the many instances where our ancestors grievously sinned but also how God our merciful Father has forgiven and showed mercy when there was humble admission of moral failure, sin, and a sincere repentance and effort to do better. The author makes this a personal moment of grace when she presents questions to ponder—how does this relate to me?

The bottom line of this challenging presentation is to recognize that we are all sinners and need God's mercy and forgiveness, which Christ brought us by his suffering and giving his very life on the cross to conquer sin, death, and the devil. We need to fall on our knees and truthfully, humbly admit our sin, and then God's mercy, love, and forgiveness overwhelm us. Then we are to share this same forgiveness and mercy with all our brothers and sisters who offend us. The great command of Jesus is, "be merciful as your heavenly Father is merciful."

Bishop Michael Pfeifer, OMI Bishop Emeritus of the
Catholic Diocese of San Angelo

If there's anything more critical to the effectiveness of a leader, it is in self-awareness. This comes through the discipline of introspection. King David had received much grace as a leader because he was willing to bare his soul before God and say, "Search me, O God, and know my heart today."

The Truth About Consequences by Merrily is a great book for self-examination. The facts about sin and consequences ring loud and clear, but the grace of God rings louder through the lives of biblical leaders, including the author's personal journey. A great handbook for soul-searching leadership.

Philip Ong, Dean, School of Leadership,
Tung Ling Bible School, Singapore

Satan sweetens his bait! He tempts with sin, while hiding the end results. The book *The Truth About Consequences* is so desperately needed by both the mature saint as well as the new believer. It aligns with the message God is highlighting in this hour—repent! Pastor, buy it! Small group leader, buy it! Youth leader, buy it! Christian, buy it! By all means, just buy it!

Rev. Dr. Jamie Morgan, Senior Pastor of Life Church, Williamstown, New Jersey, and Host of the Podcast *Fire Starter with Dr. Jamie Morgan* on the Charisma Podcast Network

Merrily does a masterful job writing this book. Obedience is not the most popular subject in the church today but definitely one of the most needed. She uncovers obedience through the Bible, from Old and New Testament Scriptures, in a warm and inspirational way. She looks at the issue of obedience in the lives of Bible characters, and also shares personal examples from her own life of the blessing that obedience brings. This book is practical as well as inspiring, a life of obedience speaks to us today as clearly as it did to those many years ago. Committed Christians will find valuable take home lessons from Merrily's excellent book.

Chad Deerman, lead pastor of Faith Alive Church, West Branch, MI, Northeast Section Presbyter, Michigan District Assemblies of God

Rev. Merrily Madero has been, and always will be, a freedom fighter. Fear not what you will face within as you are being led by this excellent heart-driven and skilled warrior. She will lead you to victory. This book contains transformational warfare wisdom. Embrace core truths from the Word of God that clear the landing sites for the Holy Spirit. You will experience the spirit and precision of a true freedom fighter as you receive God's freeing impartation from the Truths written herein. John 8:32(mev), "You shall know the truth and the truth, shall set you free."

Dr. Melonie Janet Mangum, Partners for Transformation, Aglow International Director of Transformation

Merrily has written a book that many need to read. Both new and mature believers can gain insight into the truth that there are consequences to our actions: good and bad. Merrily takes us on a journey of looking at the consequences of the actions of biblical characters so that we can gain wisdom for our lives today. This book is relevant, practical, and hopeful. I recommend you read this book, as Merrily has created an important resource for you to be able to evaluate your life and change for the better.

Dr. Rev. Diane Wigstone
Author, Speaker, Professor, Founder/President Destiny
Center, Director YWAM Hollywood

The United States of America has built a culture that rejects personal responsibility. Merrily Madero cuts right to the core of this issue. She brings the Scripture to the forefront of this issue. God holds humanity accountable for their decisions, pre-and post-cross. Grace brings even more accountable to the recipients. This book is wonderfully and poignantly written. The American church needs to read and embrace these ideas.

Dr. Scott T. Bottoms, Lead Pastor, Church at Briargate
Linda Bottoms, Asst. Church Ministries Director, Rocky
Mountain Ministries Network of the Assemblies of God

THE TRUTH ABOUT CONSEQUENCES

MERRILY MADERO

ISBN: 978-1-94429-881-4

Cover and interior design by Scot McDonald
Cover image: iStock.com/ CHIARI_VFX

LCCN: 2021904603

Printed in the United States of America

1 2 3 4 5 6 7 8 Printing/Year 22 21 20 19 18

This book is dedicated to my daughter, Leia Noelle Fecteau.

*Thank you for faith in me to write this book. I'm
grateful for the countless hours you spent helping me in the book
organization and editing, while being a full-time student. Thank you
for your encouragement, reminders of Bible stories and verses, and
your perspective to help reach a much wider audience with this book.*

*Leia, your unending quest for knowledge and desire to help
underserved populations are an inspiration to me. Congratulations
on your upcoming graduation from the Frank H. Netter MD School
of Medicine in May 2021, to become a doctor of medicine. You will do
great work for the kingdom of God!*

I'm so blessed to have you as my daughter and my best friend.

CONTENTS

FOREWORD

What do you mean there are consequences to my actions? God is a forgiving God, right? So, what's the big deal?

I had never heard anyone really talk about consequences. Then, a few years ago, Rev. Lana Heightley contacted me about including Rev. Merrily Dente Madero in our Women in Strategic Leadership mentoring roundtable that year. From that time until now, it has been a joy to journey with Merrily in her transition from serving as a colonel in the US Air Force to being an Assemblies of God ordained minister.

Because Merrily soon became involved in regular teaching opportunities in Vietnam, she would travel to Asia at least two times a year. Each time she would schedule to spend at least a week or more in my home. It was during one of my early conversations with Merrily that she mentioned she was thinking about writing a book on this topic. Immediately I encouraged her to get it done, because I was considering writing a book on the same topic. Needless to say, I am excited to see this much-needed book completed and available.

During my years of ministry, few people talked or preached about consequences, yet it is so needed for the body of Christ and beyond. Too often we rely so heavily upon God's grace, which is powerfully available, that we forget that God's justice must also be satisfied in heaven. God cannot play favorites. For example, if I put my arm on something too hot, it will be burned. Yes, it can heal, but it may result in a scar on my arm. Life is much the same way. All our choices in life will have corresponding consequences, many good, but some may leave us with undesired outcomes that we must find God's grace to live with.

This reality is not meant to frighten us, but to stir us to seek godly wisdom before making important decisions in life. Who should I marry? What about my career? Should I have sex with my partner before marriage? Critical financial decisions. Experimenting with drugs. Should I have children or not? These are choices many of us all face during our lifetime.

Personally, I chose not to marry. That was a major decision—the right one for me—that has had consequences. I will never have the joy of biological children or grandchildren. On the other side, I have thousands of spiritual children. This is just a small example of what so thoroughly and biblically presents in this book. Each page is filled with godly examples researched and supported by Scripture.

Your heart and spirit will be captivated with biblical truth as well as an opportunity for self-reflection with each chapter. While our awareness of consequences is awakened, Merrily also quickly presents God's love and provision for each of our situations. God's love and grace are more than enough.

Friends, this book is so critical for the body of Christ. So many people are struggling with guilt from perceived failures or consequences that can seem too great to handle, and for these reasons they just want to give up. Merrily stirs hope for everyone with the constant reminder that God will never leave us nor forsake us. Even with consequences in our life, God can take all of the good, the bad, and the ugly together and make something beautiful and wonderful. Never doubt the power of God available to you. Do not let your past define your future. Your future is as bright as God's promises.

Rev. Dr. Naomi Dowdy
Founder/Chancellor, TCA College, Singapore
Founder, Naomi Dowdy Mentoring and Consulting
Former Senior Pastor, Trinity Christian Centre, Singapore

ACKNOWLEDGMENTS

First and foremost, I would like to give glory to my Father God, through my Savior Jesus Christ, and thank him for the privilege to write this Holy Spirit–inspired book for him and his church.

There are many people who invested their time to take me into the next level in my walk and ministry with the Lord, and this book never would have happened without their influence in my life. They are Rev. Naomi Dowdy, Rev. Lana Heightley, Pastor David and Jennifer Black, Pastor Brady Boyd, Kathleen Dillard, the late Curt Dalaba, Pastor Chad Deerman, Rick and Julie Carter, Pastor Walt Landers, Pastors Bill and Lisa Shuler, Riaan Heyns, and David Patterson. Whether you instructed me, encouraged me, pushed me, guided me, corrected me, or helped me along God's path—thank you. For the rest of you I didn't name, thank you for being a part of my life and ministry.

A special thanks to Pam Holifield, my dear friend of over thirty-five years, who is also on my ministry board of directors, who reviewed every page, edited, and encouraged me as I wrote. Also thanks to Phil White, whose advice while serving on my ministry board of directors has kept my ministry path straight.

Diane Wigstone, thank you for monthly sessions on how to write a book. Your advice and encouragement were critical to get me started and then maintain the momentum to write.

Thanks to Karen Pickering and the entire staff at Book Villages Publishing, to guide me as I embarked on my first Christian book.

Although my parents, Frank and Ramona Dente, have been with Jesus for over a decade now, I will always be grateful of the love, faith, and integrity they lived out in their lives, which has defined me all my life.

Most of all, a huge thank you to the faithful friends and supporters of Merrily Madero Ministries, M3 International, whose prayers and financial support made publishing this book possible.

INTRODUCTION

"Dare!"

That was always my answer when playing the game Truth or Dare in my youth. We would sit in a circle and take turns deciding whether we wanted to be asked a personal question and tell a truth to the group or do a dare the group would pick. I only ever chose the dare. I never liked talking about or facing the truths in my own life, as I was a very shy and private person growing up. Since then, I may have taken the dare mindset to excess, spending most of my life pushing my physical limits by participating in extreme activities such as skydiving, base and bungee jumping, ice climbing, scuba diving, and motorcycle riding.

I also chose a daring career, serving in the United States Air Force and volunteering for several overseas deployments to Afghanistan, Haiti, and the Middle East. I served for thirty years as a mechanical engineer and leader, retiring as a colonel before the Lord called me into full-time ministry. Now I run my own nonprofit Christian ministry organization focused on leadership development in churches, Bible schools, and universities, in addition to preaching the gospel. I am also an ordained minister with the Assemblies of God church, and I go wherever the Lord sends me. I preach, teach, and serve in America and around the world, with my main focus in Southeast Asia. If you give me a microphone and a platform, I can preach and teach for hours. It is something I love to do and believe it is my primary anointing and calling from God. So, leave it to God to take me completely out of my comfort zone and direct me to write a book. There is nothing like a global pandemic to keep me home from my usually extensive overseas travel and to give me the time to finally fulfill the mandate I was given from the Lord to bring forth this book—his book.

One thing that has not changed since I was a youth playing Truth or Dare is that I still struggle to face truths in my life. I think many people feel the same way, since it can be difficult to admit certain facts to ourselves. This book is about identifying truths in the Bible and exploring how these truths intertwine with sin and consequences.

I love hearing the feel-good gospel as much as anyone, but it is time to look at the consequences many of us face from our sins. In my lifetime of church attendance, I have heard many, many messages on God's grace, which is awesome, and on God's forgiveness, which I love. However, I have yet to hear a message that directly addresses the resulting consequences we suffer when we sin. I have talked with many believers who focus only on God's forgiveness without concern for the sins they conduct. They rightly believe that when they confess and repent, God forgives and forgets, but I know there is more to it. We will always face consequences for our behavior.

We know that nonbelievers will face an eternity in hell as a consequence for their disbelief. Now it is time for all believers to realize that they, too, will face consequences for their actions on earth. We need to weigh the cost of the consequence before we sin. I know God has forgiven every sin I have confessed, and I know God is walking with me daily as I serve him. However, I also know I am enduring consequences from sinful actions in my past.

During my years of studying Scripture, what really hit me was the large number of consequences faced by most, if not all, of the men and women mentioned in the Bible. Many strong believers like Moses, who knew God, and David, a man after God's own heart, were always forgiven for their sins but still suffered consequences throughout their lives, and sometimes these consequences would stretch into future generations. This did not just happen in the Old Testament, but to believers in the New Testament as well. You will also see that not all consequences are bad, as good and faithful service to God can result in positive consequences.

Over the years, I have been asked many questions by my family, friends, and students about difficult situations in their lives. "Why do I still suffer from things I did a long time ago?" "Did the Lord truly forgive my sin when I confessed?" "Will I still suffer consequences for my sins, or is everything over once I confess and repent?" "Are all consequences bad?" "How will I endure through harsh consequences?" "Will the people who wronged me suffer consequences for their actions against me?" The good news is the Bible, the written Word of God, gives us numerous examples of consequences and will be the primary reference in this book.

I apologize in advance that this is not one of those warm, fuzzy books that tells you that "you are perfect," "everything you do is great," and "everything is acceptable under God's grace." My hope is that it will challenge you to examine the spiritual principles in your life. It will push you to take a hard look at the sins written about in the Bible, the impact of those sins, and how they relate to your life today. It will invite you to look within to determine if you are in or out of line with what God is asking of you. My primary goal for this book is for it to help you examine and more deeply understand your own spiritual life. Its purpose is to support you and give you ideas about how to continuously improve your relationship and intimacy with our loving Father God.

The primary audience for this book is today's church body, who has a basic knowledge of the Bible. Moreover, my prayer is that any person who picks up and reads this book will hear the gospel message and develop an understanding and intimacy with Jesus Christ and their loving Father God. I pray that you open your heart and spirit, and let the Holy Spirit teach you some of his truths. I encourage you to be open as you read, as I have learned that being teachable and humble are the main attitudes that have allowed me to grow in my knowledge of the Lord.

I consider chapter 1 as the doctrine of this book. It will explain my foundational premise on truth, sin, and consequences. It may seem a bit dense, but it will provide important principles you need to understand. You will see a great deal of Scripture in all chapters. I believe the Bible teaches itself, but the Lord will use me as his guide. Following this first chapter are ten chapters that will validate my premise through different biblical stories. Each chapter will typically show a different sin or action and the resulting consequences. Most importantly, those chapters end with a section showing you how to apply the key principle of the chapter to your life today. The last chapter will empower you to make any necessary changes in your life.

Get ready for a journey inward. Right now, my daughter is in her last year of medical school, so I ask her any and every question about what is going on in my now-older body. She is quick to tell me when I need to make changes to maintain my heath, and when to consult my doctor instead of obsessing about everything scary I read on WebMD. Just like we go to the doctor for checkups to make sure everything in our physical body is all right, I hope this book will provide you with a spiritual checkup.

This book is for you. Now say out loud, "This book is for me!" I want you to embrace the convictions you will feel as the Holy Spirit reveals the areas in your life that need improvement. I dare you to change your life to walk closer with our heavenly Father God, his son Jesus Christ, all through the works of the Holy Spirit. Your journey awaits.

Heavenly Father, let this book be your vessel to touch the lives and spirits of everyone who reads it. Let your Word convict, and let my words instruct, in your will and your ways. In Jesus Christ's holy name, amen.

Chapter 1

UNDERSTANDING TRUTH, SIN, AND CONSEQUENCES

Every time I look at the huge scar across my right knee, I am reminded of the consequences of my past actions. It took a while for me to accept the truth that after years of participating in extreme sports that pushed my body to its limit, I would eventually need my first total knee replacement at the age of fifty-five. Even though I no longer do most of those activities, I will always have the scar as a reminder of my fun, but dangerous, past. Similarly, it took a long time for me to admit to myself that I am a sinner, and despite God's mercy and forgiveness, I would need to endure consequences from those actions as well.

I believe many leaders in the church tend to overlook this key biblical principle in their teachings. In my experience, many believers, or those who follow Jesus Christ, do not have a clear understanding of the truth about sin and consequences. This chapter is the most important in the book, as it will provide you with the foundation upon which the subsequent chapters are built. My goal is for you to understand God's truth as it relates to sin and consequences. This chapter may convict you, but I promise it will also give you a greater understanding of how the Lord wants you to live your life during the short time we have here on this earth.

I wish I would have faced the truth about my sins and had trusted God's Word much sooner in life, instead of living for my own wishes and desires. I wish I had understood that even though I am forgiven for my sins, there would still be consequences for my actions.

What do truth, sin, and consequences have to do with each other? Are they connected in some mysterious way? Yes, they are all tied together through the Bible, the Word of God. First, we need to understand how truth is defined in the Bible. Next, we will briefly define what sin is to God. Last, we will explore how sin, or conversely, faithfulness to God, can lead to either negative or positive consequences.

Truth Is Hard

For some of us, facing the truth is difficult. Many of us would rather portray our lives as the social media dream. We desire happiness so we post fun-loving photos on social media, rather than tell the true stories of the issues that lie underneath. We like to talk about our successes but not our failures. The majority of us like to think in this way: *I am doing great; my spouse and I get along wonderfully; my kids and grandkids are doing well; I am well liked and have many friends; I am doing great in school; my boss really respects me and what I bring to our organization.* In reality, you are struggling emotionally and mentally; you and your spouse are always fighting; the kids and grandkids are a mess; you have few friends you can truly count on; you are doing poorly in school; and your boss does not respect you. These truths are hard to hear, and even harder to face. Deep down we know what is true, yet we are rarely willing to admit it to ourselves. It is important to first accept the truths so we can take action, instead of pretending our problems do not exist.

We may think we know what truth is, but let's define it for practical purposes. The basic definition of *truth* is "the body of real things, events, and facts" or "a transcendent fundamental or spiritual reality." The next step is to understand how the Bible defines *truth*. There are more than 350 references to truth or its synonyms in the New International Version (NIV) translation of the Bible. Jesus spoke often about truth in the Gospels. He mentioned *truth* or *truly* over fifty times in the Gospel of John alone. These truths clarify God's will, as it is his absolute desire for all his children to know and follow him by understanding these outlined truths.

What Does the Bible Say About Truth?

In the first chapter of the Gospel of John, he wrote, "For the law was given through Moses; grace and truth came through Jesus Christ" (John 1:17). Moses brought the law to the Israelites to define the expectations God had for his people. However, the law was, and is still, difficult for anyone to continuously uphold. The one exception to this was Jesus Christ, who lived a perfect life without sin. Jesus focused on the forgiveness of our sins, as opposed to the harsh punishments sanctioned by Israel's religious leaders toward those who broke the law. Jesus explained the truth about what his presence on earth signified for all humanity, and how his true nature and character resembled his (and our) Father God. Previously, many saw God as an enforcer or punisher. However, Jesus showed us a God who loves all his people and longs for everyone to spend eternity in heaven with him.

Jesus said, "'The reason I was born and came into the world is to testify to the truth. Everyone on the side of truth listens to me'" (John 18:37). Our purpose should be to live our lives truthfully, fully following what Jesus told us in his Word.

Jesus told his followers early in his ministry what the Father is looking for in believers:

> "Yet a time is coming and has now come when the true worshipers will worship the Father in the Spirit and in truth, for they are the kind of worshipers the Father seeks. God is spirit, and his worshipers must worship in the Spirit and in truth" (John 4:23–24).

Jesus is telling us is to be true worshipers. He is emphasizing true as opposed to false worshipers. The words "in truth" mean worshiping in a genuine, sincere way with integrity and propriety. False worshipers only make a show of worshiping. As an example, false worshipers come to church and just lip-sync the worship songs, as their minds are a million miles away from God. I am sure for many of us, this happens from time to time. We may be singing the words, but we are distracted by cares of this world. We may start critiquing the worship leader's outfit, debate where to go to lunch after church, dwell on the argument we had with our spouse or kids on the way to church, or ponder a work situation we will have to deal with during the upcoming week. Just singing the words of a worship song is not true worship to God. God is looking for those who worship with a truly focused heart, not those blindly performing a learned ritual every week. We can focus our hearts by redirecting our thoughts toward praising God, giving glory to God alone, surrendering our will to him, and doing our best not to allow outside distractions to get in the way of our special time with God. "We worship in truth because we worship what is true."[1]

Jesus spoke a great deal about truth throughout the Gospels. Over eighty times, Jesus started his preaching with, "Truly, I say to you . . ." statements. Jesus did that to get everyone's attention and to emphasize an important point he was about to make. It is like a preacher today saying, "Listen! I have some especially important words of truth you need to hear and understand." When Jesus said it twice, "Truly, truly," he really wanted to make a strong point. He had the authority as the Son of God to speak these words as God's truths. If you are looking for a good Bible study, take some time to review all the "Truly, I say to you . . ." statements Jesus spoke in the Gospels of Matthew, Mark, Luke, and John.

For those of you who do not have a strong understanding about Jesus Christ, please focus on this paragraph. One of Jesus's fundamental purposes is to be our guide on the path to our Father God. When questioned by one of his disciples, Jesus answered, "I am the way and the truth and the life. No one comes to the Father except through me" (John 14:6). Jesus is the true way to God and the true model of how we should live as believers.

Jesus also told us clearly it is only through knowing him that we can enter into a relationship with our Father God. It is so sad that our enemy, Satan, has convinced so many people there are several ways to have a relationship with God, and even a large percentage of evangelicals believe that now. As Jesus said above, he is the only way, as his truth or words in the Bible are the real truth. We are either following Jesus into heaven or following Satan down to hell. Hell is a terrible place, initially created for Satan when he revolted against God. God does not desire anyone to go to hell, but God is just, and the people who follow Satan will spend eternity with him in hell. To spend eternity in heaven, God only asks us to know and love him, to agree and confess we are sinners, to believe that his son, Jesus, was born from a virgin, died, and rose again for all of us as the perfect sacrifice, and to live our lives following his will instead of our own will.

Another key truth Jesus explained was how the Holy Spirit would help all believers. Look how Jesus referred to the Holy Spirit in John 15:26: "But I will send you the Advocate—the Spirit of truth. He will come to you from the Father and will testify all about me" (NLT). Jesus knew his time on earth was short, and his ability to explain God's truths to everyone was limited, so he explained how the Holy Spirit would come and fill the heart of every believer, both back then and today:

> "I have much more to say to you, more than you can now bear. But when he, the Spirit of truth comes, he will guide you into all the truth. He will not speak on his own; he will speak only what he hears, and he will tell you what is yet to come" (John 16:12–13).

Jesus also explained how the Holy Spirit guides us in God's truth, because the Holy Spirit is all truth, just like Jesus and our Father God. This event, the Holy Spirit coming to all believers, happened just as Jesus said it would. Shortly after Jesus Christ ascended to heaven, on the day of Pentecost, "all of them were filled with the Holy Spirit and began to speak in other tongues [or languages] as the Spirit enabled them" (Acts 2:4). Just as it is written in Acts, all believers today are filled with the Holy Spirit.

How Does Truth Relate to Sin?

One of the most quoted Bible verses about truth is "you will know the truth, and the truth will set you free" (John 8:32). Now, look at the verse in context and its relationship to sin.

> To the Jews who had believed him, Jesus said, "If you hold to my teaching, you are really my disciples. Then you will know the truth, and the truth will set you free." They answered him, "We are Abraham's descendants and have never been slaves of anyone. How can you say that we shall be set free?" Jesus replied, "Very truly I tell you, everyone who sins is a slave to sin. Now a slave has no permanent place in the family, but a son belongs to it forever. So if the Son sets you free, you will be free indeed." (John 8:31–36)

First, Jesus told believers they must know and follow his teachings to be true disciples. Once we sin, we are a slave to sin, and a slave does not have a permanent place in God's family or kingdom. We are a slave to a sin until we are freed or released through Jesus Christ, since he alone has the power and authority to do so as the Son of God. By following the words of Jesus, which as we now know are the truths of the Bible, believers will be set free from the traps of sin. When we follow and obey Jesus, we are set free from sin. This is God's truth on how to live a holy life.

Jesus also told believers about the negative effects of sin. The apostle John later wrote, "If we claim to be without sin, we deceive ourselves and the truth is not in us" (1 John 1:8). It is impossible for us as humans to never sin, so we must always be aware when we have sinned and acknowledge it. We need to examine our own heart and spirit, and if we do not find any sin, we are not being truthful to ourselves or God. It shows us an important link between truth and sin. So, knowing Jesus and his Word is knowing the truth, since Jesus and his Word are truth.

What Is Sin, and Why Do I Need to Care?

According to the Merriam-Webster Dictionary, *sin* is "an offense against religious or moral law. An action that is or is felt to be highly reprehensible. An often-serious shortcoming or fault. Transgression of the law of God. A faulty state of human nature in which the self is estranged from God."

I think of sin as anything that separates us from a holy God, and thereby goes against his perfect nature. To sin means to prioritize ourselves and our own desires over God and obedience to his Word. God hates sin because of this separation it brings between us and him. Hate may seem like a strong emotion, but the Word says, "There are six things the LORD hates, seven that are detestable to him: haughty eyes, a lying tongue, hands that shed innocent blood, a heart that devises wicked schemes, feet that are quick to rush into evil, a false witness who pours out lies and a person who stirs up conflict in the community" (Proverbs 6:16–19).

Most individuals, believers and unbelievers, acknowledge the big sins like murder and theft. But these days, it seems the rules in our society that define right versus wrong do not align closely with the commandments in the Bible. More and more ungodly behaviors are becoming acceptable, yet these behaviors are still sin to God as defined in the Bible. Sin can be fun for a time, but it will always catch up to us, and we will suffer for it.

How does God define sin? The Ten Commandments in the Old Testament are a good start.

1. You must not have any other god but me.
2. You must not make for yourself an idol of any kind or an image of anything in the heavens or on the earth or in the sea. You must not bow down to them or worship them, for I, the LORD your God, am a jealous God who will not tolerate your affection for any other gods. . . .
3. You must not misuse the name of the LORD your God. The LORD will not let you go unpunished if you misuse his name.
4. Remember to observe the Sabbath day by keeping it holy. You have six days each week for your ordinary work, but the seventh day is a Sabbath day of rest dedicated to the LORD your God. On that day no one in your household may do any work. . . . For in six days the LORD made the heavens, the earth, the sea, and everything in them; but on the seventh day he rested. That is why the LORD blessed the Sabbath day and set it apart as holy.
5. Honor your father and mother. Then you will live a long, full life in the land the LORD your God is giving you.
6. You must not murder.
7. You must not commit adultery.
8. You must not steal.
9. You must not testify falsely against your neighbor.
10. You must not covet your neighbor's house. You must not covet your neighbor's wife, male or female servant, ox or donkey, or anything else that belongs to your neighbor. (Exodus 20:3–5, 7–17 NLT)

The sad news is most believers feel these commandments are out of date and have little meaning. People do not realize they are serving the gods of wealth, success, power, and material possessions. The idols they are worshiping are not of stone, but are movie, TV, internet, and sports stars. There is no respecting God's name or dedicating any of our precious time to him. Very few people in our country give honor to their parents or those who raised them, and many ignore or send them away to be cared for by others. Although most people confess that murder is still wrong, some individuals proclaim that stealing and vandalism are OK as a means to achieve certain ends.

Adultery is very common in all media forms, and few believers still believe sex outside of marriage is a sin in God's eyes. Most do not understand that false testimony refers to lying and think that certain lies are permissible, especially if they are small. Yet all lying is a sin. And the last commandment of coveting is more prevalent than ever, as the internet makes it so easy to see what others have and strongly tempts us to desire unneeded material possessions or more social media influence. That constant comparison with others has led to suicides, careless spending resulting in debt, and jealousy of photoshopped appearances and the number likes or followers others may have. Satan has filled the world with acceptance of these sins. We can never be truly happy or fulfilled with sinful inner lives.

How Do I Know When I Sin?

Our conscience is our best guide to knowing when we sin, since we usually feel it immediately when we do something wrong. Most sins are obvious, but some sins are so common in today's world that it often surprises people when they realize these actions are sins in God's eyes. Paul wrote in Galatians about the sinful acts of the flesh that will cause us not to inherit the kingdom of God.

> The things your sinful old self wants to do are: sex sins, sinful desires, wild living, worshiping false gods, witchcraft, hating, fighting, being jealous, being angry, arguing, dividing into little groups and thinking the other groups are wrong, false teaching, wanting something someone else has, killing other people, using strong drink, wild parties, and all things like these. I told you before and I am telling you again that those who do these things will have no place in the holy nation of God. (Galatians 5:19–21 NLV)

These words are pretty clear, and they validate the Ten Commandments and add to it. Acting in these sinful ways is outside the character of God and is sinful behavior.

Paul also told us to stay away from people who

> will love only themselves and their money. They will be boastful and proud, scoffing at God, disobedient to their parents, and ungrateful. They will consider nothing sacred. They will be unloving and unforgiving; they will slander others and have no self-control. They will be cruel and hate what is good. They will betray their friends, be reckless, be puffed up with pride, and love pleasure rather than God. They will act religious, but they will reject the power that could make them godly. Stay away from people like that! (2 Timothy 3:2–5 NLT)

When we spend too much time with people who act in these ways, we will eventually accept and even mimic that behavior. It is good to help sinners repent and turn their lives into a closer walk with Jesus Christ, but do not let them influence you.

Here is one more list from Paul about those who are living in sin. I love the way he wraps up this particular passage:

> Don't you realize that this is not the way to live? Unjust people who don't care about God will not be joining in his kingdom. Those who use and abuse each other, use and abuse sex, use and abuse the earth and everything in it, don't qualify as citizens in God's kingdom. A number of you know from experience what I'm talking about, for not so long ago you were on that list. Since then, you've been cleaned up and given a fresh start by Jesus, our Master, our Messiah, and by our God present in us, the Spirit. (1 Corinthians 6:9–11 MSG)

We all have the opportunity to be cleansed from our sins and given right standing with God. When we call on the name of Jesus, ask for-giveness, repent, and change our ways, we are cleansed from all our sin and given a fresh start. Only then will we achieve true happiness and fulfillment in our spirit.

When we feel convicted about an action we have taken or words we have spoken, it is the Lord's way of letting us know, through the Holy Spirit, that we have sinned. When we are close to God, we feel that conviction or hear "a still small voice" tell us when we sin. However, as we drift away from God, that voice and conviction become harder to hear, and we can fall away from the Lord and start living only for ourselves.

None of us is perfect; we all sin. The Bible says, "For all have sinned and fall short of the glory of God" (Romans 3:23). When we sin, it puts up a wall between us and God, which leads to death, or separation from God. We will all die, so the question is, Will we spend eternity in heaven with Jesus and our Father God, or in the terrible "lake of fire" with Satan?

It is appropriate for us to examine our lives, but this does not mean we should judge others. Though the Bible mentions circumstances where believers should confront the sins of others, for the most part, we should never judge another person's sin. God knows their hearts, their motives, and their actions; we do not. We should hate the sin but love the sinner. Many believers walk away from God because of the negative actions, words, and judgment of other believers. We should make sure that never happens.

So just as sin leads to death, Jesus left heaven to save us from death, or permanent separation from God. We have hope in a relationship and eternity with our Father God, through Jesus's death on the cross. Jesus lived a perfect life with no sin, and so he became the perfect sacrifice to cleanse our sins. Look how the apostle Paul explained this concept.

> When Adam sinned, sin entered the world. Adam's sin brought death, so death spread to everyone, for everyone sinned. . . . For the sin of this one man, Adam, caused death to rule over many. But even greater is God's wonderful grace and his gift of

righteousness, for all who receive it will live in triumph over sin and death through this one man, Jesus Christ. Yes, Adam's one sin brings condemnation for everyone, but Christ's one act of righteousness brings a right relationship with God and new life for everyone. Because one person disobeyed God, many became sinners. But because one other person obeyed God, many will be made righteous. God's law was given so that all people could see how sinful they were. But as people sinned more and more, God's wonderful grace became more abundant. So just as sin ruled over all people and brought them to death, now God's wonderful grace rules instead, giving us right standing with God and resulting in eternal life through Jesus Christ our Lord. (Romans 5:12, 17–21 NLT)

These verses explain what it means to have a sin nature, an innate nature to sin because of Adam. The good news is God gave us a way to overcome our sins in the form of a Savior, Jesus Christ, who made the ultimate sacrifice and died in our place for our sins. That is what grace is all about, unmerited benevolence by God. So, when we believe, God's grace takes the place of our sins. We all have the gift of grace when we believe, but we need to confess our sins to bring us back into a relationship with God.

What Should We Do When We Sin?

The Word of God is very clear. "If we confess our sins, He is faithful and just to forgive us our sins and to cleanse us from all unrighteousness" (1 John 1:9 NKJV). The first word in that verse, *if*, makes our forgiveness conditional. We cannot go around sinning without recourse. We may see others around us sin all the time. Yet, we should not measure our actions against the world as we know it. God is not judging us based on the world's standards, but we are judged by his commandments.

Sometimes we sin and we wait expectantly for God to strike us with a bolt of lightning. When that does not happen immediately, we think we have gotten away with our sin. Unfortunately, that is never the case. God always knows what is going on in our lives. He not only knows our actions, but our thoughts and motives as well. God "alone examines the motives of our hearts" (1 Thessalonians 2:4 NLT), and "people may be pure in their own eyes, but the LORD examines their motives" (Proverbs 16:2 NLT). We cannot hide from God.

Sadly, the more we sin, the more we become numb to it and its impact on our lives. We will be judged on our motives, careless words, and sinful actions. We will stand alone when we face God at judgment day, and what everyone did around us will have zero impact on our judgment. The good news is, God will forgive our sins if and when we confess them to him. Then we are cleansed from all unrighteousness, or sin in our lives, since this is promised by God, who is faithful in his promises to us who believe and follow him. "God can maintain his perfect character and yet forgive us because of the perfect and righteous sacrifice of Jesus, His own son."[2]

When you hear that voice of conviction, or know in your heart you have sinned, confess it immediately. Do not wait for church on Sunday or your prayer time to ask the Lord for forgiveness. Confess it right away. When you confess your sin, it brings you back into a relationship with God. "And I will forgive their wickedness, and I will never again remember their sins" (Hebrews 8:12 NLT). Once you confess your sins to God, he forgives your sins, then forgets them, and it is like they never existed. Oftentimes, we are the ones who remind God about our sin. We do not need to keep confessing the same original sin over and over again. Once you stop doing that sin and ask for forgiveness, it is forgotten by God.

Once you confess your sins, you need to determine what actions led you to sin and stop that behavior, or stay away from those temptations. If you do not genuinely change your behavior, you will soon find yourself doing the same sins over and over again. We all need to repent.

Not only did John the Baptist speak often about repentance, but Jesus did as well. The first words Jesus spoke as he began his ministry were

"Repent of your sins and turn to God, for the Kingdom of Heaven is near" (Matthew 4:17 NLT). Stop sinning. Stop lying, gossiping, cheating, and treating others poorly. Ask the Holy Spirit to convict you when you sin, and then focus on ways to change that behavior. We need to remember to forgive ourselves, too, as that is usually the hardest part.

God is quick to forgive you when you repent with a true heart; however, that does not stop Satan from holding your sins over your life. Satan will try to limit your work for God's kingdom by telling you because of your past sins you are not worthy to serve God. That is a lie, so do not let Satan hold those sins over you. Jesus forgives all sins, no matter how bad. If you do not know Jesus Christ and would like to, remember these ABCs: Admit you are a sinner and have made mistakes. Believe in Jesus, that he died on the cross for you, and God raised him from the dead on the third day. Confess you need a Savior and follow Jesus with all your heart.

We all sin and fall short of the glory of God. The good news is, when we confess our sin, repent, and change our lives, we become true believers and will spend eternity in heaven with Jesus and our Father God. However, that doesn't mean we won't face consequences due to those sins.

Why Will We Face Consequences?

What happens when you drive twenty miles per hour over the posted speed limit? Are you breaking the law? Yes. What happens if a police officer with a radar gun catches you going that fast? In most cases, you will get a speeding ticket and have to pay a large fine as a consequence for your unlawful action, and it should teach you to slow down. Some of you may be skilled at talking your way out of a speeding ticket, but that has never happened for me. If you receive too many tickets, your right to drive will be revoked. Regardless if you are caught or not, it was still unlawful for you to speed. If you continue to drive over the speed limit, eventually you will get caught and face the consequences. The same is true for us when we sin.

Paul tied this to understanding and respecting authority, with a resulting punishment when we break the rules.

> Everyone must submit to governing authorities. For all authority comes from God, and those in positions of authority have been placed there by God. So anyone who rebels against authority is rebelling against what God has instituted, and they will be punished. For the authorities do not strike fear in people who are doing right, but in those who are doing wrong. Would you like to live without fear of the authorities? Do what is right, and they will honor you. The authorities are God's servants, sent for your good. But if you are doing wrong, of course you should be afraid, for they have the power to punish you. They are God's servants, sent for the very purpose of punishing those who do what is wrong. So you must submit to them, not only to avoid punishment, but also to keep a clear conscience. (Romans 13:1–5 NLT)

Paul spoke clearly about punishment for wrong actions and behavior when we break the rules of our governing authorities. In comparison, when we sin and break God's commands, he always knows and holds us accountable. When we confess, we are forgiven, but we will often face some sort of consequences or punishment for those sins. I believe the more willful we are in our sins against God, the greater the consequences we will face.

What Are Consequences?

Most dictionaries define *consequence* as the outcome or effect of something that happened previously. I define *consequence* as "a justified result from a deliberate action." Consequences tie most often with our choices. If we choose to do the right thing, we will face a good consequence. However, if we choose to do the wrong thing, or commit a sin, it will typically lead to negative consequences. In contrast, obedience to God's commands leads to good consequences.

Usually, we think of consequences as negative, as most of us can remember a time when we were children and had to face consequences for bad behavior. Remember your parents warning you to play nice with your siblings/friends or you would get a time-out, or you would be grounded if you got home too late? Breaking those rules probably resulted in a consequence of some sort. These days, taking away mobile devices or games seems to be the negative form of consequence to reasonably, effectively correct many behaviors of children.

Several verses in the Bible talk about consequences related to sin and inappropriate behavior. When I see two to three Scripture references in the Bible about a specific subject, I take them to be an absolute truth in God's Word. Here are just a few of them:

> They will bear the consequences of their sin. (Numbers 9:13)

> "But I will punish you in accordance with the [appropriate] consequences of your decisions and your actions," says the LORD. (Jeremiah 21:14 AMP)

> You will bear the consequences of your lewdness and your detestable practices, declares the LORD. (Ezekiel 16:58)

All three of these verses are tied with the Israelites' sinful behavior, followed with consequences when they did not turn from their sinful ways. The same is true for us today, as we will suffer consequences for our sins. Happily, many more Bible verses tell us about the rewards we will receive for faithful and obedient godly behavior.

> Now if you obey me fully and keep my covenant, then out of all nations you will be my treasured possession. (Exodus 19:5)

> His master replied, "Well done, good and faithful servant! You

have been faithful with a few things; I will put you in charge of many things. Come and share your master's happiness!" (Matthew 25:21)

A faithful person will be richly blessed. (Proverbs 28:20)

Whatever you do, work at it with all your heart, as working for the Lord, not for human masters, since you know that you will receive an inheritance from the Lord as a reward. It is the Lord Christ you are serving. (Colossians 3:23–24)

And without faith it is impossible to please God, because anyone who comes to him must believe that he exists and that he rewards those who earnestly seek him. (Hebrews 11:6)

Our journey through the following chapters will highlight the consequences that some of our favorite Bible characters endured for their sinful or faithful actions. Each chapter details a Bible story, examines what positive or negative actions occurred, and then explains a key point that you can learn to apply to your own walk and relationship with God. Blessings as you continue this journey.

Chapter 2

HOW ADAM AND EVE'S FIRST SIN IMPACTED US ALL

often ponder what it would have been like to be the first man or woman created by God. How glorious it must have been to live in such an idyllic place, with an abundance of fresh water and food hanging off the trees. I wonder how it felt to have the privilege of naming all the animals and creatures, while peacefully tending a beautiful garden with a partner created just for you, and, most of all, to walk and talk daily with our Father God. It was paradise—or at least we think it was. Yet, it was not enough for Adam. He disobeyed the only rule he had been given.

This story, as with all stories, begins with God. He created the earth, skies, oceans, lands, plants, and animals, and then he created Adam, the first man. "The LORD God took the man and put him in the Garden of Eden to work it and take care of it. And the LORD God commanded the man, 'You are free to eat from any tree in the garden; but you must not eat from the tree of the knowledge of good and evil, for when you eat from it you will certainly die'" (Genesis 2:15–17).

Adam was given one task, to tend the Garden of Eden. Then, God gave him just one command: do not eat from the tree of the knowledge of good and evil, which was just one of the many fruit trees in the garden. You would think that would be a pretty easy command for Adam to follow, and he did so for a while.

After some time, God formed the first woman from one of Adam's ribs, as a suitable equal partner to tend the garden. It appeared Adam was happy, for he said, "This is now bone of my bones and flesh of my flesh; she shall be called 'woman,' for she was taken out of man" (Genesis 2:23).

Who really was the serpent, the next character in this story? There is a debate among scholars as to who this serpent was and what it represented. For this book, we will look to the book of Revelation, which states, "He seized the dragon, that ancient serpent, who is the devil, or Satan, and bound him for a thousand years" (Revelation 20:2).

Adam and Eve did not realize the serpent was their enemy, just like most people today do not realize how the devil presents himself to us in seemingly innocuous forms. Satan, in the form of the serpent, did everything he could to get Adam and Eve to go against God's will for their lives. The serpent tempted Eve by causing her to doubt God's whole truth and giving her only a half-truth. The serpent questioned Eve by saying, "Did God really say, 'You must not eat from any tree in the garden?'" (Genesis 3:1). There is no biblical record of Eve hearing directly from God concerning the tree of the knowledge of good and evil, so we do not know exactly what Adam told Eve, and in what context he told her. Did Adam make a big deal about it, or did he just casually mention it one day as they were working in the garden?

Eve replied back to the serpent, "We may eat the fruit of the trees of the garden; but of the fruit of the tree which is in the midst of the garden, God has said, 'You shall not eat it, nor shall you touch it, lest you die'" (Genesis 3:2–3 NKJV). Eve did not even give the tree the same name that God told Adam: the tree of the knowledge of good and evil. Then, Eve added they were not to touch it or eat the fruit. Was it Adam or Eve who inappropriately added to God's commands? Adding to God's Word quickly gets us into trouble.

The serpent continued to plant doubt in Eve's mind by saying, "You won't die! . . . God knows that your eyes will be opened as soon as you eat it, and you will be like God, knowing both good and evil" (Genesis

3:4–5 NLT). The serpent deceived Eve when he told her she would not die. Eve probably did not even know what it meant to die. The serpent misled Eve into thinking God was denying her and Adam some special revelation, and if they ate the fruit, they would become equal with God.

Eve saw the fruit of the tree as desirable, so she ate it. Then "she also gave some to her husband, who was with her, and he ate it" (Genesis 3:6). Wait a minute! When did Adam join this conversation? We do not know if Adam joined Eve and the serpent as they headed to the tree, or if he was with them the entire time. At no point did Adam jump into the conversation and correct the disinformation from the serpent, nor did Adam mention they were doing something God told him not to do, nor did he take any action to protect Eve from sinning. Adam just ate the fruit given to him by Eve. I think Eve often gets the brunt of the blame for this sin, even though it was Adam who received the warning from God and did not correct Eve or challenge the serpent during this conversation.

Life immediately changed for Adam and Eve now that their eyes were opened to the knowledge of good and evil, and they realized they were naked and exposed. Adam and Eve knew they had disobeyed God's direction, so they were afraid to see him. They hid from God during their usual daily time of fellowship, so they not would have to be confronted by him for their sin. When God called out to them, Adam replied, "I heard you in the garden, and I was afraid because I was naked; so I hid" (Genesis 3:10). Like Adam, we cannot hide our sins from God, as he sees and knows all our sins. God said to Adam, "Who told you that you were naked? Have you eaten from the tree that I commanded you not to eat from?" (Genesis 3:11). As in all cases, God knew exactly what Adam's sin was without having to ask, but it was a test of integrity.

When God confronted Adam, he blamed Eve. Look at what Adam said: "The woman you put here with me—she gave me some fruit from the tree, and I ate it" (Genesis 3:12). Adam blamed God for putting the woman in the garden, and then did not accept any responsibility for his sin of eating the fruit. That was terribly wrong for Adam to do. When we sin, exactly how and when we repent are vitally important. We need to confess immediately, accept responsibility for our actions, and repent in such a way that we turn completely from that sin and do not commit it again. When asked, Eve blamed the serpent for deceiving her, but at least she confessed eating the fruit of the forbidden tree.

● ● ● ●

What Was Adam and Eve's First Sin?
Disobedience

By eating that fruit, both Adam and Eve were disobedient to God and his will for their lives, and the price of their sin resulted in severe consequences.

▶▶▶ The Consequences

As soon as God confronted Adam and Eve, he imposed consequences on both of them and on the serpent. "Then the Lord God said to the serpent, 'Because you have done this, you are cursed more than all animals, domestic and wild. You will crawl on your belly, groveling in the dust as long as you live. And I will cause hostility between you and the woman, and between your offspring and her offspring. He will strike your head, and you will strike his heel'" (Genesis 3:14–15 NLT).

The serpent must have had a very high standing in the Garden of Eden to have been able to speak and move around the garden with Adam and Eve. So, this consequence reduced him to the lowest form of animal, living on its belly in the dust, as his curse. The hostility God described above between the serpent, or Satan, and mankind occurs in both physical and spiritual realms. Physically, man and woman will always stand above the serpent, but the serpent can cause painful bites to humans. Spiritually, a constant battle between Satan and mankind is now afoot. It foreshadowed how Christ would come from a women's seed and would be the one to eternally defeat

Satan. Satan still has the ability to wound us, and he does that by getting us to focus on worldly pursuits, in contradiction to God's commands. However, when we know, trust, and follow our Lord, Jesus Christ, we can withstand Satan's temptations and live for our Father God.

"Then [God] said to the woman, 'I will sharpen the pain of your pregnancy, and in pain you will give birth. And you will desire to control your husband, but he will rule over you'" (Genesis 3:16 NLT). Eve would be the first mother on the earth, but her consequences were that the joy of bringing forth new life through childbirth would now come with intense pain.

Next, initially Eve was Adam's equal partner in tending the garden. This new command from God gave Adam spiritual authority. Please note, this verse in the Bible does not give husbands the right to abuse or control their wives, but husbands should set the example for their wives and families in serving God. These were the consequences from Eve's sin of disobedience and is now passed on to all women.

Adam heard directly from God and still disobeyed him, so I believe Adam was held more accountable than Eve and received harsher consequences. "And to the man he said, 'Since you listened to your wife and ate from the tree whose fruit I commanded you not to eat, the ground is cursed because of you. All your life you will struggle to scratch a living from it. It will grow thorns and thistles for you, though you will eat of its grains. By the sweat of your brow will you have food to eat until you return to the ground from which you were made. For you were made from dust, and to dust you will return'" (Genesis 3:17–19 NLT).

Adam's life of leisure tending the garden was over. Instead of taking a stand for God, Adam followed the crowd. Neither Adam nor Eve would be able to continue their intimate fellowship with God, walking together in the garden. Their sin forced a separation between them and a holy God. From this point on, there would be hardship and trials in order for them to survive, especially since they were kicked out of the Garden of Eden. Instead of paradise, there would be struggle, pain, sickness, and death.

● ● ●

Are We Still Suffering Those Same Consequences?

Mankind is still suffering from those consequences. This initial sin brought to all of us a nature or desire to sin. Plus, women still suffer pain in childbearing. Mankind still toils and labors in work to survive. We all suffer from hardships and trials, pain, and sickness. Mankind must choose between an eternity in heaven with God or an eternity in hell with Satan, based on whom they serve. These consequences are all directly related to Adam and Eve's original sin. The good news is Jesus Christ came to the earth to bring all willing people back into fellowship with our Father God if they follow him. In contrast, those who follow Satan and his evil ways will end up in hell with him. These consequences, given to Adam and Eve, have been passed down through every generation until today.

How Does This Relate to Me Today?

We must realize that Satan wants to deceive every one of us, just like he did Eve. We need to keep on constant guard against Satan's treachery. These days, Satan has convinced most of the world he does not exist, which allows him to operate without limits in many areas. When disaster strikes, people are quick to blame God instead of realizing mankind's nature to sin allows Satan to pursue his path of destruction.

Satan wants believers to doubt God's promises, to think we can have it all without any restraints. How often have we heard these lies whispered to us by Satan? "You should have a nicer car or better job like your neighbor." "You really deserve a new outfit, even though your credit cards are maxed out." "Just try those drugs once; you will not get hooked." "You can have one more drink tonight and will still be OK to drive home." "No one will see you take that item or do that illegal action." How many times have you joined in on sins just because everyone else was doing them? It is often easier to join in than to take a stand and do what is right and honorable.

I love the classic depiction of a person pondering a decision with a devil on one shoulder and an angel on the other. That is very close to what goes on every day in the spiritual realm, as Satan tries to get you to do the wrong thing while the Holy Spirit tries to get you to do the right thing. Those voices are real, and as believers, we need to recognize both the voice of Satan and the voice of the Holy Spirit, so we can follow the way of the Lord and ignore Satan. The Bible warns us to "be alert and of sober mind. Your enemy the devil prowls around like a roaring lion looking for someone to devour" (1 Peter 5:8). Satan continues to tempt and devour generation after generation with the same sins.

Just like we are enduring the same consequences as Adam and Eve, consequences from sin can pass down through generations. We are warned, "For I, the Lord your God, am a jealous God, punishing the children for the sin of the parents to the third and fourth generation of those who hate me" (Exodus 20:5). Many have been inflicted with consequences passed down from their forefathers and foremothers. Our sins, therefore, can cause consequences to be passed down to our children and even grandchildren, as generational curses can continue unabated. There is an abundance of evidence in the fields of genetics and psychology that addiction, mental illness, and even domestic abuse or violent tendencies seem to be passed down from generation to generation. When children are born, they have a mixture of genes from each of their parents and are often susceptible to the same disorders. Additionally, when children witness sinful behavior, they will likely behave in the same way. Whether these curses are associated with genetics or environment during upbringing is beyond the scope of this book, but I am sure many of us have stories we can recount.

In my family, I was told how alcoholism had ruined my grandfather's life. His addiction cost him his family and many jobs, and he died at a young age. Then, the same thing happened to my only sister. She started drinking when she was in her early teens and could never get free of it, no matter how many times we tried to help her. She died just before she turned forty-three from cirrhosis of the liver. I have engaged in significant spiritual warfare to break that curse in my family and ensure it does not pass to me, my daughter, or her children.

There is hope for us, as God also tells us he shows "love to a thousand generations of those who love me and keep my commandments" (Exodus 20:6). We have a loving Father who wants us and all our future generations to follow him. We can break generational curses by calling out the curse by name and commanding it to be broken in the name of Jesus Christ. If you would like to know more about doing this, several excellent books on breaking generational curses are on the market today. So, if you feel like there is a generational curse that is running through your family, stop what you are doing right now, and break that curse in the name of Jesus Christ.

Questions to Ponder

▶ How often do I go along with the crowd instead of taking the moral high ground?

▶ When was the last time I was disobedient to a command from God? Do I recognize when Satan is trying to tempt me into sin?

▶ What generational curses are being passed down in my family that need to be broken?

The Truth About Consequences

Sin can result in generational consequences (Adam and Eve).

Chapter 3

DON'T MAKE A MOSES MISTAKE

Can amazing followers of God make life-changing mistakes? Yes, as we will see in the story of a man who met God face-to-face, then made a mistake that would cost him dearly. Moses is one of the most interesting and important Old Testament characters in the Bible. The events throughout his life are synopsized in more chapters of the Bible than any person except Jesus. The story of Moses starts in Exodus 2, continues through all of Leviticus and Numbers, and finishes in the final chapter of Deuteronomy. Moses is credited with writing each of those books in addition to Genesis. He was an incredible leader and prophet, but he, like all humans, made mistakes, and we can learn much from them.

The Story of Moses

Moses's life has been depicted in many big-screen movies and is a favorite among Sunday school stories. Most of us can recall the image of him as a baby floating in a basket down the Nile River to escape certain death by Pharaoh's decree, only to be rescued and raised as a prince of Egypt by the pharaoh's daughter. The Bible records that Moses ran from his glamorous life in fear after killing an Egyptian guard who was beating a Hebrew slave. We are told in Exodus how God appeared to Moses forty years later while he tended sheep in Midian and called him to return to Egypt to rescue the Hebrew people. Who can forget that classic movie scene with Charlton Heston as Moses, confronting Pharaoh to let God's people go, followed by the parting of the Red Sea to escape the pharaoh's chariots?

Once the Hebrew people were safe, Moses had a second face-to-face meeting with God on Mount Sinai to receive the Ten Commandments. Moses was a great servant and leader for God, and he is identified in the list of individuals commended for their faith in the book of Hebrews. "It was by faith that Moses, when he grew up, refused to be called the son of Pharaoh's daughter. He chose to share the oppression of God's people instead of enjoying the fleeting pleasures of sin. He thought it was better to suffer for the sake of Christ than to own the treasures of Egypt, for he was looking ahead to his great reward" (Hebrews 11:24–26 NLT).

Moses may have been an incredible man of God, but did he live a sinless life after meeting God face-to-face twice? No, just like us, Moses had to overcome sin in his life.

Leading the Israelites

Moses had a difficult job as the leader of over three million Israelites, in addition to flocks and herds of animals. He did this for twenty-four hours a day, seven days a week, for forty years of wandering in the desert in miserable conditions. Moses had to face endless grumbling and quarreling as the Israelites went through numerous trials and challenges. We will review just two of these scenarios and show how Moses's careless sin resulted in a consequence he had to endure for the rest of his life.

After 430 years of slavery in Egypt, the Israelites were free. They witnessed many miraculous events: multiple plagues against Egypt, the parting of the Red Sea to escape Pharaoh's pursuing chariots, a tower of fire to see at night, a guiding cloud to follow by day, and manna from heaven to live on. Yet, the Israelites complained to Moses.

Just a few weeks after leaving Egypt, Moses and the Israelites were on their way to Mount Sinai as God had commanded:

The whole Israelite community set out from the Desert of Sin, traveling from place to place as the LORD commanded. They camped at Rephidim, but there was no water for the people to drink. So they quarreled with Moses and said, "Give us water to drink." Moses replied, "Why do you quarrel with me? Why do you put the LORD to the test?" But the people were thirsty for water there, and they grumbled against Moses. They said, "Why did you bring us up out of Egypt to make us and our children and livestock die of thirst?" Then Moses cried out to the LORD, "What am I to do with these people? They are almost ready to stone me." (Exodus 17:1–4)

Whenever the situation got tough, not only did the people grumble and argue, they also questioned their decision to leave their life of slavery. They only remembered their previous homes and water wells, and not the whip and confinement of slavery. This was not the first nor the last time Moses would cry out to the Lord for help concerning the Israelites, who were quick to forget the many miracles God performed on their behalf.

The Lord gave Moses very specific instructions. "'Go out in front of the people. Take with you some of the elders of Israel and take in your hand the staff with which you struck the Nile, and go. I will stand there before you by the rock at Horeb. Strike the rock, and water will come out of it for the people to drink.' So Moses did this in the sight of the elders of Israel. And he called the place Massah and Meribah because the Israelites quarreled and because they tested the LORD saying, 'Is the LORD among us or not?'" (Exodus 17:5–7).

Moses obeyed God's command and struck the rock. The result was plenty of water for all the people and livestock. This story took place just a few weeks after leaving Egypt. Now fast-forward through forty years of wandering in the desert. The Israelites returned to the same location and experienced the same drought conditions and lack of water.

> Now there was no water for the community, and the people
> gathered in opposition to Moses and Aaron. They quarreled with
> Moses and said, "If only we had died when our brothers fell dead
> before the LORD! Why did you bring the LORD's community
> into this wilderness, that we and our livestock should die here?
> Why did you bring us up out of Egypt to this terrible place? It
> has no grain or figs, grapevines or pomegranates. And there is
> no water to drink!" (Numbers 20:2–5)

These complaints were made by a new generation of Israelites that
had been born in the desert. They had not experienced the slavery their
parents and grandparents had, yet still they challenged Moses and his
brother, Aaron (who was now Israel's high priest and helped Moses
lead the people). How tiring that must have been for Moses. Where
was the trust in the Lord who provided for them during all those years
in the desert?

When Moses and Aaron went to the Lord about the water situation,
this time the Lord told Moses to speak to the rock and the water would
pour out. However, Moses did not do as the Lord commanded. "Moses
took the staff from the LORD's presence, just as he commanded him.
He and Aaron gathered the assembly together in front of the rock and
Moses said to them, 'Listen, you rebels, must we bring you water out of
this rock?' Then Moses raised his arm and struck the rock twice with
his staff" (Numbers 20:9–11).

Moses yelled at the people, then instead of speaking to the rock
as the Lord commanded, Moses struck the rock not once, but twice.
Maybe he felt adding a dramatic element would get the people's attention
and make a lasting impact. I think Moses had some anger issues after
watching the Israelites grumble and test God time and time again. Was
he weary after forty years of wandering in the desert, fed up with the
people, or just having a bad day? None of those were valid excuses for
his sinful behavior.

The water still came out of the rock by God's loving grace and care for his people; however, both Moses and Aaron were in trouble with the Lord.

• • •

What Sins Did Moses and Aaron Commit?
Dishonoring God and Acting Out in Anger

Moses's action was rash, impatient, and disobedient, and he made God out to be an angry God, not the holy God who loved and cared for his people in times of trouble. Aaron did not step in at any point to correct this sinful behavior.

▶▶▶ The Consequences

Even though Moses and Aaron were faithful leaders, the Lord was quick to confront both of them for their sinful actions and proclaim harsh consequences: "The Lord said to Moses and Aaron, 'Because you did not trust in me enough to honor me as holy in the sight of the Israelites, you will not bring this community into the land I give them'" (Numbers 20:12).

• • •

The Promised Land was a pledge given to Abraham, so that his descendants would someday settle in an abundant land. God told Moses, and all the Israelites at Mount Sinai, the time to settle in the Promised Land was coming soon. Moses knew the Lord was a holy and righteous God, not an angry or vengeful God. But by yelling at the people and adding his own dramatic flair of striking the rock twice, Moses painted God in a negative light.

After spending forty years with the Israelites wandering the desert, neither Moses nor Aaron would set foot in the Promised Land. Why such a harsh consequence? Through Moses's words and actions, he put the focus on himself and not God. When Moses spoke to the people, he said, "Must *we* bring you water out of this rock?" rather than "must

God." Moses and Aaron assumed the role of provider for the Israelites instead of rightfully proclaiming the Lord as primary provider. In doing this, Moses dishonored God in front of the Israelites, and his rash actions were a direct act of disobedience against the command God had given him.

In Aaron's case, his sin was a lack of action to correct Moses. Just a short time later, Aaron's time on earth came to an end. For his sin of rebelling against God, Aaron suffered the consequence of neither seeing nor entering into the Promised Land. However, Aaron was still forgiven and loved by God, and his family line would serve as priests for the Israelites. "Only the descendants of Aaron serve the LORD as priests, and the Levites alone may help them in their work" (2 Chronicles 13:10 NLT). Aaron left a lasting legacy, as his son took over and carried on this priestly line for the Israelites.

As the Israelites were ready to step into the Promised Land, Moses would face his consequences for the actions at Meribah. Here is what the Lord said to Moses:

> Go up into the Abarim Range to Mount Nebo in Moab, across from Jericho, and view Canaan, the land I am giving the Israelites as their own possession. There on the mountain that you have climbed you will die and be gathered to your people, just as your brother Aaron died on Mount Hor and was gathered to his people. This is because both of you broke faith with me in the presence of the Israelites at the waters of Meribah Kadesh in the Desert of Zin and because you did not uphold my holiness among the Israelites. Therefore, you will see the land only from a distance; you will not enter the land I am giving to the people of Israel. (Deuteronomy 32:49–52)

This one sinful action by Moses also cut short his time on earth. The Bible says, "Moses was a hundred and twenty years old when he died, yet his eyes were not weak nor his strength gone" (Deuteronomy 34:7).

His early death was a direct consequence to his sin at Meribah, but these closing verses in Deuteronomy remind us that Moses was still a godly man: "There has never been another prophet in Israel like Moses, whom the Lord knew face to face. The Lord sent him to perform all the miraculous signs and wonders in the land of Egypt against Pharaoh, and all his servants, and his entire land. With mighty power, Moses performed terrifying acts in the sight of all Israel" (Deuteronomy 34:10–12 nlt).

Moses committed one rash act and faced a tough consequence for his sin. As a leader for the Israelites, Moses had a great responsibility, so he also faced greater consequences. He performed years of faithful service to God and to the Israelites and was one of the few who met face-to-face with God. Did God still love Moses? Yes. Was he a great leader and prophet? Yes. Did God ever forgive Moses for his rash behavior? Yes. But both Moses and Aaron still had to live and die with the consequences from this one careless action.

How Does This Relate to Me Today?

All of us have experienced how one wrong word or deed can have devastating lifelong consequences. Being caught while driving under the influence of alcohol or drugs can be costly in terms of finances, work, and even the lives of those who are with us. Stealing from a store or a work location can have career-ending impacts that stay on your record forever. An inappropriate relationship leading to an affair may cost you your family.

Like many of you, I have personally witnessed many of these unfortunate scenarios in close family members and friends. One of my friends attended a work party to celebrate a company award. After having a few drinks, he correctly decided to take a cab home to be safe. However, soon afterward his boss called and scolded him for leaving him without a ride home. My friend was new to the company as a recent college graduate and felt pressured to go back to the party and give the boss a ride home. Sadly, he made the unfortunate mistake of jumping in his roommate's car to get his boss and was pulled over for driving under the influence.

In addition to personal and legal ramifications, having the DUI charge on his record impacted his security clearance at work, and he was let go from the company. That one careless mistake cost him his livelihood.

It can often be difficult to weigh clearly the costs and rewards of a seemingly minor action when we are in the heat of a moment, especially when we may feel a great deal of outside pressure. However insignificant an improper action may feel at the time, it can still lead to lifelong consequences.

We all need to be vigilant to ensure we are not committing careless acts that lead to sin. The Bible tells us to "lead a life worthy of your calling, for you have been called by God" (Ephesians 4:1 NLT). Some of you have been called to serve God in the secular world, and you need to remember all your words and deeds will reflect on your life as a follower of Jesus. Nonbelievers will be quick to judge your work and behaviors, and will look closely to see if you are a good example and live a righteous life. Also, as believers, we know what God expects of us, so when we knowingly sin against God's commands, we are held more accountable. I feel believers are held to a higher standard since we know God's commands, and the consequences we face will be tougher than those of nonbelievers.

I also believe that those of us who are called to ministry positions are held to an even higher standard. We should fulfill God's commands in all ways and situations, and model his commandments to the best of our ability. I take my calling as a teacher very seriously, especially since James wrote, "Not many of you should become teachers, my fellow believers, because you know that we who teach will be judged more strictly" (James 3:1). I weigh that statement with every class I teach and sermon I preach.

All of us face times when we are weary and struggling. However, we need to remember we are a light for our Father God and his son, Jesus Christ. One careless word or action, especially in front of those who look to us for wisdom and guidance, can have lasting effects. Do not let one sinful action cost you something you hold dear. Do not allow a sin to cost you something that could impact you the rest of your life. We all know of an individual whose sin has had lasting consequences. Do not let that happen to you. Don't make a Moses mistake.

Questions to Ponder

▶ How often do I say careless words or act with rash behavior?

▶ What consequences am I suffering from right now due to careless actions in my past?

▶ How can I improve my words and actions so I do not commit careless sins?

The Truth About Consequences

One careless sin can lead to lifelong consequences (Moses and Aaron).

Chapter 4

IS GOD WITH ME AS I WANDER?

Most of the Old Testament focuses on the exciting and intriguing stories of the Israelites—their history, trials, and triumphs as God's chosen people. These descendants of Abraham were a troublesome lot for the most part, and just could not seem to remain faithful to God, no matter how many miracles he performed for them. What delayed the Israelites' journey into the Promised Land? We will delve into that story, the resulting consequences, and how the Lord took care of them throughout their—and our—wandering in the desert.

In the Desert

Not long after their incredible rescue from slavery in Egypt and receiving the Ten Commandments at Mount Sinai, the Israelites headed toward the Promised Land of Canaan. However, the land was not just sitting vacant. It was a prosperous land filled by many people of different races who had already built houses and cities, and planted numerous fields of crops. Stepping into a fully prepared homeland was part of the blessing the Israelites were to receive from God.

Here was God's direction to Moses: "Send out men to explore the land of Canaan, the land I am giving to the Israelites. Send one leader from each of the twelve ancestral tribes" (Numbers 13:2 NLT).

Moses told the scouts to report back whether the land was fertile or poor, flat or hilly, with or without forests. They also were to bring back whatever fruit they found growing there and to check if the cities were unwalled or fortified, if the people were strong or weak, and how many there were. After forty days, the twelve scouts reported back to Moses and the people that the land flowed with milk and honey, the people were powerful, and the cities were fortified. The grapes they brought back were so abundant that they had to be carried on a pole between two men. Sadly, most of the scouts then began to speak in fear of the vast numbers of people living there and the strength of their walled cities. They did not trust in the promise from God that the land was already theirs.

Yet not all of the twelve scouts doubted God's promise. Two of them, Caleb and Joshua, took a stand and trusted that God would help them to take possession of the land. The ten remaining scouts spread fear among the Israelites: "'We can't attack those people; they are stronger than we are.' And they spread among the Israelites a bad report about the land they had explored" (Numbers 13:31–32).

The Israelites looked at the situation in terms of their own strength, not in terms of the strength of the God who had freed them from Egypt. God had already told them the land was theirs, and that he would go before them as they conquered the land. Once again, the Israelites rebelled against Moses and Aaron, and even began talking about going back to Egypt.

> One of the righteous scouts, Joshua, provided a positive report and reminded the people to trust in God: "The land we passed through and explored is exceedingly good. If the LORD is pleased with us, he will lead us into that land, a land flowing with milk and honey, and will give it to us. Only do not rebel against the LORD. And do not be afraid of the people of the land, because we will devour them. Their protection is gone, but the LORD is with us. Do not be afraid of them" (Numbers 14:7–9).

These powerful words should have reminded the Israelites to believe and trust in God, instead of giving in to their fear. God was with the Israelites, not with the Canaanites, who had lost God's protection due to their heinous sins. Alas, the Israelites were afraid and threatened to stone Joshua. Thankfully, the Lord stepped in to save Joshua, but condemned the people. "The LORD said to Moses, 'How long will these people treat me with contempt? How long will they refuse to believe in me, in spite of all the signs I have performed among them?'" (Numbers 14:11).

● ● ●

What Was the Sin of the Israelites?
Lack of Faith and Distrust in God's Promises, Testing God, and Treating God with Contempt

Moses had to plead with the Lord so he would not eliminate all the Israelites and start over with a new nation from Moses's family line. Moses asked for forgiveness for the people, which the Lord granted.

> The LORD replied, "I have forgiven them, as you asked. Nevertheless, as surely as I live and as surely as the glory of the LORD fills the whole earth, not one of those who saw my glory and the signs I performed in Egypt and in the wilderness but who disobeyed me and tested me ten times—not one of them will ever see the land I promised on oath to their ancestors. No one who has treated me with contempt will ever see it." (Numbers 14:20–23)

This was a long list of sins against the Israelites. In just the short time from departing Egypt, the Israelites tested God ten different times. God refers to their contempt, or lack of respect or reverence for him. Despite that, God still forgave them once Moses petitioned on their behalf. Despite God's forgiveness, the Israelites still faced severe consequences for these sins.

▶▶▶ The Consequences

The Israelites would never enter or even see the Promised Land.

> "For forty years—one year for each of the forty days you explored the land—you will suffer for your sins and know what it is like to have me against you." I, the LORD, have spoken, and I will surely do these things to this whole wicked community, which has banded together against me. They will meet their end in this wilderness; here they will die." . . . These men who were responsible for spreading the bad report about the land were struck down and died of a plague before the LORD. (Numbers 14:34–35, 37)

● ● ●

God took immediate action against the ten scouts who gave the negative report, and they died swiftly of a plague. The rest of the Israelites were destined to wander in the desert for forty years, until everyone who believed the negative report died. Shortly after these events, the Israelites once again changed their mind and decided they wanted to enter the Promise Land.

> But Moses said, "Why are you now disobeying the LORD's orders to return to the wilderness? It won't work. Do not go up into the land now. You will only be crushed by your enemies because the LORD is not with you. When you face the Amalekites and Canaanites in battle, you will be slaughtered. The LORD will abandon you because you have abandoned the LORD." But the people defiantly pushed ahead toward the hill country, even though neither Moses nor the Ark of the LORD's Covenant left the camp. Then the Amalekites and the Canaanites who lived in those hills came down and attacked them and chased them back as far as Hormah. (Numbers 14:41–45 NLT)

The Israelites' one and only attempt to enter the Promised Land, prior to the Lord's timing, was disastrous and not attempted again.

In the last chapter, we saw how one careless action by Moses and Aaron led to lifelong consequences. The Israelites now faced a similar fate, but that is not the end of the story. What happened during those forty years wandering in the desert? How much did the Israelites have to suffer? Was God with them during those years of struggle?

The Bible tells us, "The LORD your God has blessed you in all the work of your hands. He has watched over your journey through this vast wilderness. These forty years the LORD your God has been with you, and you have not lacked anything" (Deuteronomy 2:7).

As they endured their consequences, God still loved and provided for them. The Israelites had to endure the consequences of wandering for forty years in the desert for their sins, yet God was with them providing for them the entire time: "By day the LORD went ahead of them in a pillar of cloud to guide them on their way and by night in a pillar of fire to give them light, so that they could travel by day or night. Neither the pillar of cloud by day nor the pillar of fire by night left its place in front of the people" (Exodus 13:21–22). God provided this constant show of presence and protection throughout their journey. He also blessed them with everything they needed to survive. Look at what he told the Israelites just before they entered into the Promised Land:

> Remember how the LORD your God led you all the way in the wilderness these forty years, to humble and test you in order to know what was in your heart, whether or not you would keep his commands. He humbled you, causing you to hunger and then feeding you with manna, which neither you nor your ancestors had known, to teach you that man does not live on bread alone but on every word that comes from the mouth of the LORD. Your clothes did not wear out and your feet did not swell during these forty years. Know then in your heart that as a

man disciplines his son, so the LORD your God disciplines you. (Deuteronomy 8:2–5)

There were other reasons the Israelites faced trials in the desert, besides punishment for past sins. Those forty years became a period of total trust and dependence on God as he alone provided for them. God fed them manna, or bread from heaven, every day, teaching them that he was the only true source they could rely on. They would face many challenges and temptations once they entered into the Promised Land, so God taught them humility. The Lord also reminded his people how he took care of them, their health, and their clothing the entire time they wandered in the desert.

At the end of those forty years, the Israelites finally were brought into the Promised Land:

> Observe the commands of the LORD your God, walking in obedience to him and revering him. For the LORD your God is bringing you into a good land—a land with brooks, streams, and deep springs gushing out into the valleys and hills; a land with wheat and barley, vines and fig trees, pomegranates, olive oil and honey; a land where bread will not be scarce and you will lack nothing; a land where the rocks are iron and you can dig copper out of the hills. (Deuteronomy 8:6–9)

The fulfillment of a promise made long ago to Abraham had finally come to pass. The Israelites sinned but were forgiven. Even though they faced severe consequences for those sins, God was with them every step of their journey.

How Does This Relate to Me Today?

What I really love about the Bible is that it does not sugarcoat anything. It lays bare the sins and many faults of God's people. When the

Israelites engaged in all manner of sins, they were recorded in the Bible. Why? So we can learn from them today. We need to be careful not to cast judgment on them, without looking at our own walk with God and our struggles to remain faithful to his commands. When we think we have it tough, we only need to look at these Old Testament stories and realize our life today is not so bad.

God needed to prepare the Israelites for the great challenges they would endure once they entered into the Promised Land. They would face tremendous temptations, as they would see the extremely sinful practices of the people they would conquer. The Israelites had witnessed firsthand some of the most amazing miracles ever recorded. Yet, they quickly forgot about God's power when faced with trials. This happens with believers today as well.

We need to know God so we can remember his promises when we face challenges. We should not be focused on the world, frightened by the news, and distracted by social media during our trials. We need to trust his plan for our lives and not our own plans. I believe God has a perfect plan and path for our lives, just like he did for the Israelites. "'For I know the plans I have for you,' declares the LORD, 'plans to prosper you and not to harm you, plans to give you hope and a future'" (Jeremiah 29:11).

In order to stay on God's perfect path, we need to stay close to him and hear the directions he has for us. To know what God wants for us, we need to spend time with him and have a relationship with him, just as we need to do with our spouse, families, and friends. Most spouses would not appreciate only seeing you once a week for an hour, then having no communication with you throughout the rest of the week. That is usually what most believers give to God—one hour on Sunday mornings. In order for any relationship to have a deep connection, it requires effort on our part and an investment of time. As with all relationships, the more time we invest, the stronger the relationship will become.

Jesus told us the benefits of knowing him and hearing his voice: "I am the good shepherd. The good shepherd sacrifices his life for the sheep. . . . I know my own sheep, and they know me. . . . My sheep listen to my voice; I know them, and they follow me. I give them eternal life, and they will never perish. No one can snatch them away from me" (John 10:11, 14, 27–28 NLT).

Finding time every day to read God's Word, then spending time in prayer are key to knowing Jesus and hearing his voice. Prayer does not just mean a long list of things we want God to do for us. It also means taking some quiet time to listen and hear what he wants from us as well. When we are not hearing from God every day, we can easily step onto the wrong path, which will bring us farther away from God. This will result in negative consequences, just like it did for the Israelites.

I faced a similar situation in my own life. I did not trust God, was disobedient to his direction, and suffered consequences from it. Thankfully, God stayed with me and helped me throughout my entire ordeal.

Many years ago, I attached myself to a close family member and made several financial investments. At one point, I felt a strong prompting by the Lord through the Holy Spirit to separate myself and my investments from that individual. At the time, I was an immature believer, not confident I had heard clearly from the Lord, especially because in the worldly sense, everything looked and seemed great. I reasoned that God did not understand the situation, and I knew what was best. Plus, it would have been very embarrassing to walk away, as several of my friends had encouraged me to invest with this member of my family.

However, God knew better. Soon after I ignored his prompting, the situation took a sharp turn for the worse, and I eventually ended up more than $154,000 in debt. I made a huge mistake not trusting in God. If I had only listened to the Holy Spirit! I quickly asked God for forgiveness and repented for my sins, but I still had to suffer the consequences of paying off that excessive debt. Many friends and family members encouraged me to file for bankruptcy; however, after a great deal of time in prayer, I heard the Lord tell me the debt was my responsibility, and he would guide me in paying it off. In retrospect, I can see now how the Lord was with me during my entire struggle, even after forgiving me for my sin of ignoring his prompting.

The Lord sent me some amazing roommates to help cover my rent, and he gave me wisdom in maintaining a strict budget. The Lord also provided me financial opportunities to make additional money, and several times I received unexpected financial blessings from others. It was amazing how during that time neither my old car nor anything major broke down, requiring costly repairs. I had no unexpected expenses, and it was as if things did not wear out—just like the Israelites. It may have taken nine long years to repay that debt, but the Lord blessed and provided for me the entire time.

God always wants what is best for us. However, just as a parent disciplines their children so they learn right from wrong, the Lord disciplines us as well. The Bible tells us, "My child, don't reject the LORD's discipline, and don't be upset when he corrects you. For the LORD corrects those he loves, just as a father corrects a child in whom he delights" (Proverbs 3:11–12 NLT). He will put us through trials because he loves us and he wants us to grow to depend on him, not the world.

Most importantly, we need to remember that he is with us as we walk through dark times that may come from our past sins. He is also with us if we are just having a bad day, feeling guilty about the way we treated someone, or sad about a loss in our lives. It is during those periods that we should thank him for the many blessings he has given us: a sunny day, a roof over our heads, a job, our health, close friends and/or family members. Regardless of our circumstances, we do not need to fret and worry. When we walk with him and follow his commands, we will lack nothing. God is always with you, and he will continue to provide for you throughout your consequences.

Questions to Ponder

▸ When am I closest to God—during the good times or the bad times?

▶ How am I focusing too closely on worldly roadblocks and obstacles in my life, instead of trusting in God and the gifts he has given me to achieve my goals?

▶ How is God providing for me in the midst of my consequences?

The Truth About Consequences

The Lord provides for us in the midst of our consequences (the Israelites in the desert).

Chapter 5

ARE ALL CONSEQUENCES BAD?

Now it is time to look at some positive consequences. The previous chapter centered on the sin of the Israelites for treating God with contempt after believing the ten negative scouts who explored the Promised Land. Their consequence involved wandering for forty years in the desert until all who doubted God would perish; however, the Lord provided for them the entire time. Did the two scouts who took a stand for the Lord suffer the same punishments as everyone else? We will see how these two men became heroes for trusting in God and were the only two Israelites who had left Egypt to enter into the Promised Land.

The Scouts

Most scholars agree the scouts were not the head of their tribes but were one of the tribe's leaders. Each tribe likely chose a well-respected and godly middled-age man who was healthy enough to take an extended journey. There must have been a sense of excitement as they entered the land, preparing for God's promise. However, only two of the twelve scouts, Caleb and Joshua, remembered God's promises, while the rest lost their faith in God.

At first, there was a great deal of joy as the scouts saw the beautiful lands, abundant crops, sturdy houses, and fortified cities. But often when believers are separated from their spiritual family, they begin to lose faith and instead focus on the world. Is that what happened to the ten scouts who developed an attitude of fear? They started believing there was no way a group of wandering ex-slaves could go head-to-head with the fierce people of Canaan, so they passed their disbelief on to all the Israelites upon their return. However, the two faithful scouts, Caleb and Joshua, kept their eyes focused on God and rejoiced in the promises God had given to them.

They came back to the Israelites with hope and joy at the abundant lands the Lord was giving them. After the negative report by the ten scouts, "Caleb silenced the people before Moses and said, 'We should go up and take possession of the land, for we can certainly do it'" (Numbers 13:30). Caleb took a stand in faith, believing in the promises of God and trusting they were able to take the land he had given them. However, Caleb was countered by the other ten scouts: "But the men who had gone up with him said, 'We can't attack those people; they are stronger than we are.' And they spread among the Israelites a bad report about the land they had explored. They said, 'The land we explored devours those living in it. All the people we saw there are of great size. . . . We seemed like grasshoppers in our own eyes, and we looked the same to them'" (Numbers 13:31–33).

Undeterred, Joshua stood up with Caleb to remind the people to trust in God, and they "tore their clothes and said to the entire Israelite assembly, 'The land we passed through and explored is exceedingly good. If the LORD is pleased with us, he will lead us into that land, a land flowing with milk and honey, and will give it to us. Only do not rebel against the LORD. And do not be afraid of the people of the land, because we will devour them. Their protection is gone, but the LORD is with us. Do not be afraid of them'" (Numbers 14:6–9).

Despite these encouraging words, the crowds grew violent and the Lord had to intervene so Joshua would not get killed. We reviewed the sins of distrust and contempt the Israelites committed in the last chapter, and the resulting consequences of forty years wandering in the desert until all those who stood with the ten disbelieving scouts would perish and never see the Promised Land.

How did these events impact Caleb and Joshua? Right after the ten unfaithful scouts were struck down, Moses reported, "Of the men who went to explore the land, only Joshua son of Nun and Caleb son of Jephunneh survived" (Numbers 14:38).

Caleb, the Faithful Scout from Judah

Of the twelve scouts, Caleb was the first to take a stand for God. What a great man of faith to stand firm in God's promises, especially when confronted by the multitudes of Israelites. The Lord was quick to recognize this faithfulness:

> "My servant Caleb has a different attitude than the others have. He has remained loyal to me, so I will bring him into the land he explored. His descendants will possess their full share of that land" (Numbers 14:24 NLT).

Caleb would not die in the desert with the other Israelites, but would enter into the Promised Land. He was a warrior and fought for many years to secure the inherited land that was promised to all the Israelites. Caleb was in his eighties when they arrived in the Promised Land, and he was one of the few men to fight until all the tribes received their land. He would receive the part of the land he personally explored as his reward and inheritance to pass on to his family.

The first important point is Caleb did not live in fear. It must have been difficult for Caleb to watch all his friends and family members die during those forty years in the desert, but his faith never faulted. He was blessed to receive the land that he scouted out forty-five years earlier, which I believe was the desire of his heart. Next, Caleb did not sit around and wait for his enemies to depart. He trusted the promise of God that the land was his and stepped out in faith to take his land, as he was directed by God. Caleb fought with all the Israelites to the end, and once he received his inheritance, the land rested from war (see Joshua 14:6–15). It is not written in the Bible when Caleb died, though we know he lived longer than Joshua, as there are references to Caleb in Judges 1:12 after Joshua's death.

Joshua, a True Servant Leader

As a humble servant leader and warrior, Joshua has always been one of my favorite men in the Bible. He started with humble beginnings as Moses's helper, aide, and all around go-to guy. We first hear of Joshua shortly after the Israelites left Egypt. Exodus 17:8–14 tells the story of how the Amalekites attacked the Israelites as they were heading toward Mount Sinai. Moses sent Joshua out to lead the fight. The story shows how it was God who defeated the Amalekites, using Joshua and his men as a tool to ensure his will. The men were only successful while Moses's arms were raised up, and they would falter when he lowered them. Ultimately, God provided the victory.

We also know that Joshua accompanied Moses up Mount Sinai when he received the Ten Commandments, and it was Joshua who alerted Moses about the noise from the people as they sinfully made the golden calf. We also know Joshua "had been Moses' aide since youth" (Numbers 11:28). So, it is not surprising that he was selected as the scout from the tribe of Ephraim to go into the Promised Land.

When Moses was told he would not enter into the Promised Land due to the consequence of his sin, the Lord directed Joshua to be the next leader for the Israelites. Joshua had served Moses and the Lord humbly and faithfully for forty years, and the Lord rewarded him with the position of leader among the Israelites. Joshua led Israel through the difficult task of driving out the inhabitants who were living in Canaan. Joshua fought with every tribe and settled in his inherited land in Timnath Serah in the hill country of Ephraim. As a true servant leader, he was the last to receive his piece of the Promised Land. He made no demands and accepted what was given to him.

Joshua lived to be 110 years old, and he led the people well: "Israel served the Lᴏʀᴅ throughout the lifetime of Joshua and of the elders who outlived him and who had experienced everything the Lᴏʀᴅ had done for Israel" (Joshua 24:31). What a great testimony to his role as an amazing spiritual leader for the people of Israel to have followed the Lord completely under his leadership. We all should strive for that kind of reward for our own walk and ministry.

● ● ●

Caleb and Joshua's Faith in Action
Trust, Obedience, and Faithful Service to God

▶▶▶ The Positive Consequences

Out of several million Israelites who departed Egypt, only Caleb and Joshua entered the Promised Land. They remained faithful to God's promises and trusted in him completely. They were rewarded with health, vigor, and long lives and were able to defeat their enemies until all of Israel was settled, and there was peace in the land. Both of them received a great inheritance, a piece of the Promised Land for their future generations.

● ● ●

How Does This Relate to Me Today?

I believe faith requires action. When God tells us to do something, we need to do it. Faith does not mean sitting around and waiting for God to change all the circumstances. We must step out in faith to do what God calls us to do to receive our good consequences or rewards. Do you have faith and courage like Caleb and Joshua to take a stand or fight a battle against those who doubt God?

Many people will never fulfill their God-given calling because they do not step out in faith. Throughout my time following Jesus, I have met many people who, like me, felt strongly called by the Lord to serve in the role of a pastor or overseas missionary. I think we would all agree this is a difficult calling. The difference between those of us who succeeded as pastors and missionaries and those who did not seems to come down to our choice to be active or passive in fulfilling this calling. Every person faces different obstacles, and it takes hard work, perseverance, and, hardest of all, sacrifice to overcome many of them. I cannot count the number of hours and dollars I have invested into pursuing the ministry path the Lord has put me on. I have been more fortunate than most to have fantastic mentors like Pastor Naomi Dowdy and Rev. Lana Heightley, who have opened numerous ministry doors for me. With great mentors and guidance from the Lord, I have been able to build up my ministry and secure teaching and preaching opportunities around the world. I am also adapting to new challenges every day as COVID-19 has turned most of my overseas teaching opportunities into Zoom sessions.

I have heard many good excuses for choosing an easier path than full-time ministry—the timing never "felt" right, worries about the effect on family, uncertainty about where financial support would come from, and some who just did not want to give up a comfortable life to jump into something unknown. I will be the first to admit how scary the choice can be. But in the end, I believe those who do whatever it takes to follow in God's perfect path will reap rich rewards, and those who choose the opposite path will lose many rewards and blessings that God had planned for them. To take a stand to trust and obey the Lord has not been easy in my experience, but I have always been rewarded when I listened and obeyed.

It can be intimidating to try to think of our whole lives, our future, and plan them to be in perfect obedience to God. Our lives are made up of a series of small daily decisions, and our path is determined by how we approach these. Even when decisions seem insignificant, we can still seek God's direction to keep on the right track, and he will help us in ways we did not think were possible. His Word tells us, "The Lord will guide you continually, giving you water when you are dry and restoring your strength" (Isaiah 58:11 NLT).

I always loved leading short-term overseas mission trips, and one of my dreams was to one day serve in Nepal. My heart ached to visit the people and to serve God in that country. One year, I was part of an amazing short-term mission trip to the Philippines. During that trip, the host organization announced the next year over Thanksgiving week they would go to Nepal for the first time. I was ecstatic; however, I felt a check in my spirit not to sign up or pay the deposit right away. Several times I went to the Lord, and I sensed he did not want me to go on the trip. Finally, as the deadline to sign up was quickly approaching, I went away for a time of prayer and fasting so I could hear clearly from the Lord. I strongly felt the Lord tell me it was not the right time to go on the trip, but that there would be another opportunity to do mission work in Nepal in the future.

This was difficult at the time, but I listened. Very unexpectedly, a last-minute work crisis ended up occurring right before Thanksgiving week, and I would have had to cancel the trip if I had gone ahead and scheduled it. The Lord knew the timing for me to go to Nepal that year was wrong, and I saved a lot of money by not canceling an international trip at the last minute. As promised, the Lord opened the door for me to serve in Nepal a couple years later, with significant ministry impacts, and I formed many lifelong friendships. It was a great reward for obeying God and waiting on his timing.

We, too, can receive good consequences and rewards for our faithful service when we follow God's commands and his will for our lives. God's Word says, "The LORD rewards everyone for their righteousness and faithfulness" (1 Samuel 26:23). We do that by developing a relationship with him so he can communicate to us through his Holy Spirit. We are righteous and faithful when we listen and do God's will for our lives. We also know that God "rewards those who earnestly seek him" (Hebrews 11:6). Does that reward mean wealth and riches? Maybe for a few, but more importantly, God promises a life of fulfillment as we carry out his work here on earth. I believe we will see some of those good consequences while we are still here on this earth, but some of the rewards we will see only when we get to heaven and see Jesus face-to-face.

Questions to Ponder

▶ Have I ever taken the time to ask God what he wants me to do today?

▶ Do I step out in faith when God tells me to do something big?

▶ What rewards have I received for obedience and faithful service?

The Truth About Consequences

Expect rewards for faithful service to God (Caleb and Joshua).

Chapter 6

DON'T LET YOUR SIN MULTIPLY

We often learn our greatest lessons from our greatest failures. King David's adulterous relationship with Bathsheba was his greatest failure. This is one of the hardest stories in the Bible to read, as we see the downward spiral of a great man of God. The good news is this story has a huge message of redemption, and we see David's genuine repentance and the forgiveness he received from the Lord. However, appropriate consequences still followed.

The Story of David

If you are someone like me, who always roots for the underdog, then the story of David is probably one of your favorites. David had to overcome a great deal of adversity and hardship throughout his life, and it all started as the youngest of eight sons, often being overlooked by his own father, Jesse. A prime example was when the prophet Samuel came to Jesse's home to anoint one of his sons as the next king of Israel, and David was not even brought forward to be considered. Fortunately, Samuel kept asking about other sons until Jesse summoned David from tending the sheep in the fields. Once David arrived, the Lord told Samuel, "Rise and anoint him; this is the one" (1 Samuel 16:12). Samuel immediately anointed David to be Israel's next king over all his older brothers. However, it would take many more years before David would receive the crown.

His experience as a lonely shepherd fending off fierce beasts, like lions and bears, gave him the needed experience to take on the giant Goliath with just a sling and stones. This act of bravery earned him a promotion into King Saul's palace and marriage to his daughter. David's military successes led to Saul's extreme jealousy. David spent many years on the run from King Saul and could have killed him on multiple occasions; however, David proclaimed he would never be the one to take King Saul's life. Finally, when Saul was wounded in battle and took his own life, David was crowned king over all of Israel, and he reigned for forty years.

David was a warrior, king, musician, and poet. He wrote seventy-three psalms, and the Bible highlights his musical skill with the harp. He had an intimate relationship with the Lord: "God testified concerning him: 'I have found David son of Jesse, a man after my own heart; he will do everything I want him to do'" (Acts 13:22). Those are precious words that we should hope the Lord also will say about us.

The Lord promised David his lineage would produce the Messiah, the expected king and deliverer of the Jews (see 2 Samuel 7:1–17). Both Mary and Joseph, Jesus's parents, were from David's lineage (see Matthew 1:1–17; Luke 3:23–38). After David received the crown of Israel and the promise of a great lineage from God, one would think he would continue to be a righteous man. However, after receiving great victories, David drifted from the Lord and got trapped in an escalating web of sin.

The Affair

This particular story begins with David remaining behind in Jerusalem while his armies went off to war. David was a warrior, and it was customary for him to be with his soldiers on the battlefield. There is no reason given why David stayed behind. Was David feeling lazy? Enjoying the comfortable palace over the rough conditions out on the battlefield? Was it his pride? Did David feel he was "above" fighting now that he was king? David's first problem was he was not where he was supposed to be—fighting with his army. This led to a very big temptation. "Late one afternoon, after his midday rest, David got out of bed and was walking on the roof of the palace. As he looked out over the city, he noticed a woman of unusual beauty taking a bath. He sent someone to find out who she was, and he was told, 'She is Bathsheba, the daughter of Eliam and the wife of Uriah the Hittite'" (2 Samuel 11:2–3 NLT).

We, as readers, have many questions at this point. The first one is, What was Bathsheba doing bathing out in the open, and in view of the king's terrace? Did she do it intentionally to get noticed, or was she completely blameless? If it was a common practice in those days, there is no record of David witnessing other women bathing on their roofs. Bathsheba grew up around David, as her grandfather Ahithophel was a longtime counselor of David, and her father, Eliam, had fought with David. So, perhaps she had hoped she would one day become one of David's wives, but instead she was married to one of David's mighty warriors. Was Bathsheba unhappy with Uriah? Since the couple had not yet conceived a child, perhaps this weighed heavily on Bathsheba. The Bible does not give us the answers to these questions.

Uriah had fought by David's side throughout his previous struggles with King Saul (see 1 Chronicles 11:41) and was now fighting for him against the Ammonites. You would think this information would give David pause out of respect for a longtime faithful comrade. However, that news did not stop him from committing a significant sin of the flesh. "Then David sent messengers to get her; and when she came to the palace, he slept with her. She had just completed the purification rites after having her menstrual period. Then she returned home" (2 Samuel 11:4 NLT).

How did David drift away so easily from God's commands and commit this sin? He struggled for years while he was on the run from King Saul and remained close to God. Now that he was living the good life, did he stop spending time with God? Was he distracted by numerous material goods and possessions he received as king, or overindulged by servants who brought him anything he wanted? Oftentimes when we fight a long battle and the struggle is over, we feel that we no longer need God, so we take our eyes off him. Is that what happened to David? Perhaps he witnessed and learned this type of behavior when he lived in the palace with King Saul. It was not uncommon in those days for kings to bring many women into their harems, but not usually married women. David already had many wives and concubines at this point, but that did not stop him from committing the sin of taking another man's wife.

• • •

What Was David's First Sin?

Adultery

David and Bathsheba committed the sin of adultery, as they were both married to others. Since Bathsheba had just completed her menstrual period before coming to David, she was not already pregnant by her husband. Additionally, Uriah had been off fighting in the war for many months prior to this event. We do not know how long she stayed with David in the palace. We find no biblical record that she was raped or taken against her will, as that is usually recorded. We also do not know what David may have promised Bathsheba concerning their relationship.

It does not take long for the consequence of this sinful relationship to become evident. Bathsheba's pregnancy caused huge problems for her, as adultery was punishable by death under Jewish law (see Leviticus 20:10; Deuteronomy 22:22). Additionally, by this point, several servants at the palace were aware of this indiscretion by David.

David knew he was in trouble, so he used false pretenses to bring Uriah back home. Instead of confronting his sin, David started down a path of deception to cover up his initial sin of adultery. David thought if Bathsheba's husband was back in town, then Bathsheba's pregnancy could be covered up by regular husband-and-wife sexual relations. However, we find out that Uriah was a dedicated and honorable man.

> Then he told Uriah, "Go on home and relax." David even sent a gift to Uriah after he had left the palace. But Uriah didn't go home. He slept

that night at the palace entrance with the king's palace guard. When David heard that Uriah had not gone home, he summoned him and asked, "What's the matter? Why didn't you go home last night after being away for so long?" Uriah replied, "The Ark and the armies of Israel and Judah are living in tents, and Joab and my master's men are camping in the open fields. How could I go home to wine and dine and sleep with my wife? I swear that I would never do such a thing." "Well, stay here today," David told him, "and tomorrow you may return to the army." So Uriah stayed in Jerusalem that day and the next. Then David invited him to dinner and got him drunk. But even then he couldn't get Uriah to go home to his wife. Again he slept at the palace entrance with the king's palace guard." (2 Samuel 11:8–13 NLT)

What Was David's Second Sin?

Deception

Uriah was an incredibly loyal man, especially as a foreigner fighting for David and the Israelites. David tried twice to get Uriah to go home to his wife, Bathsheba. However, Uriah did not focus on fleshly pursuits, even though he had every right to go home, relax, and sleep with his wife. Uriah's thoughts were on his fellow soldiers and honoring the Ark of the Covenant. David's sinful deception did not work.

David told one lie after another to cover his initial sin of adultery. Then, he tried every deception he could think of to get Uriah to go and sleep with Bathsheba, to cover the adultery. We can only imagine how panicked David was at this point. It would not be long before Bathsheba's pregnancy would become obvious. David became desperate, so what did he do?

What Was David's Third Sin?

Murder

So the next morning David wrote a letter to Joab and gave it to Uriah to deliver. The letter instructed Joab, "Station Uriah on the front lines where the battle is fiercest. Then pull back so that he will be killed." So Joab assigned Uriah to a spot close to the city wall where he knew the enemy's strongest men were fighting. And when the enemy soldiers came out of the city to fight, Uriah the Hittite was killed along with several other Israelite soldiers. (2 Samuel 11:14–17 NLT)

How desperate David was to have a very loyal soldier killed to hide his own sin. When David was notified about Uriah's death, he was relieved. Uriah had stood by David throughout his toughest times, yet we do not even see any remorse from David. His initial sin of adultery led to an escalation of sin.

David did choose to maintain a degree of honor through this situation and made Bathsheba his wife after Uriah's death. But the Lord saw each one of David's sins, and he would pay the price for them. It took the prophet Nathan's rebuke before David confronted his own sin.

▶▶▶ The Consequences

The Lord God laid out a harsh message for David through the prophet Nathan:

> "I anointed you king of Israel and saved you from the power of Saul. I gave you your master's house and his wives and the kingdoms of Israel and Judah. And if that had not been enough, I would have given you much, much more. Why, then, have you despised the word of the LORD and done this horrible deed? For you have murdered Uriah the Hittite with the sword of the Ammonites and stolen his wife. From this time on, your family will live by the sword because you have despised me by taking Uriah's wife to be your own. This is what the LORD says: 'Because of what you have done, I will cause your own household to rebel against you. I will give your wives to another man before your very eyes, and he will go to bed with them in public view. You did it secretly, but I will make this happen to you openly in the sight of all Israel.'" (2 Samuel 12:7–12 NLT)

The Lord emphasized David had received much, but God would have given David much, much more if he had not committed such sins and if he had repented on his own accord. When we read the rest of 2 Samuel and 1 Kings 1–2, we see all these painful consequences play out. Several of David's sons rebelled against him, and there was infighting among the family throughout David's life. One of David's sons declared himself king, so David had to go into hiding with his immediate family but left ten of his concubines to care for the palace. To prove he should be made king, David's son Absalom "slept with his father's concubines in the sight of all Israel" (2 Samuel 16:22), thus fulfilling another one of David's consequences. This was a tough list of consequences for David, but worthy of the crimes and sins he committed. David's sins multiplied from adultery to deception, culminating in murder.

● ● ●

We do not know what blinded David to these sins through the birth of his child with Bathsheba. It took a confrontation from Nathan before David would admit his sins and turn his life around. The good news was David quickly confessed his sin before the Lord: "David confessed to Nathan, 'I have sinned against the LORD.' Nathan replied, 'Yes, but the LORD has forgiven you, and you won't die for this sin. Nevertheless, because you have shown utter contempt for the word of the LORD by doing this, your child will die'" (2 Samuel 12:13–14 NLT).

David pleaded with the Lord to save his son, but death still came as God said. Fortunately, the Lord gave David and Bathsheba another son, Solomon (see 2 Samuel 12:24–25). We see the strong influence of Bathsheba as she reminded David before his death of his promise to her that Solomon would be king (see 1 Kings 1:11–30). The Lord loved Solomon, and he went on to be the next king and a part of the lineage of Jesus the Messiah (see 1 Kings 1–2).

How Does This Relate to Me Today?

We can all think of a time when one small lie got us into trouble. On occasion, that one lie led to several more lies that may have continued for years so we could save face. Sometimes we say the same lie so often, we begin to believe it. It is a downward spiral in which most of us have found ourselves caught at one time or another. Even today, I am tempted at times to tell a quick and easy lie, rather than explaining the true reasons why I cannot do something when asked. Thankfully, the Holy Spirit always convicts me to speak the truth. We often make excuses for our behavior, and though consequences may not be immediately evident, there is no doubt they will follow. We saw how David's sin multiplied. This will happen in our own lives, as sins can and will escalate.

As a former commander in the military, I was granted authority under the Uniform Code of Military Judgment (UCMJ) to review and determine certain punishments for wrongful actions of military personnel under my command. I had the authority to levy several formal disciplinary actions, such as reducing enlisted personnel in rank, denying promotions, levying fines, or requiring additional work duty during their off hours. I told every military member who came to me for judgment that if they were honest, accepted responsibility for their actions, and would take steps to correct their behavior, I would factor that into my ruling. Many would accept responsibility and strive to do better, thus receiving a lesser punishment. However, there were a few individuals who sustained their lies, blamed everyone but themselves, and continued to deny the charges against them, even when there was solid proof of their violations. When this happened, strict and severe punishment was given according to the appropriate protocol. Oftentimes they started a downward spiral in their military careers, which impacted the rest of their lives. Those individuals often continued to commit more and more violations, with additional charges against them that resulted in a quick exit from the military and a lifelong Bad Conduct Discharge on their record. It was always troubling to witness those downward spirals.

Often after we receive great victories in our lives, the enemy easily catches us with our guard down and we sin, which can escalate rapidly. When we get wrapped up in these types of cascading sins, it may be difficult to break free by ourselves. Paul gave us hope when he wrote, "No temptation has overtaken you except what is common to mankind.

And God is faithful; he will not let you be tempted beyond what you can bear. But when you are tempted, he will also provide a way out so that you can endure it" (1 Corinthians 10:13).

You can overcome temptation in your life. Do not let sin tempt you or continue to escalate as it did for David. I believe we fare better when we confront these sins in ourselves, ask forgiveness and repent, and trust in the Lord. If we do not correct our own sinful behaviors, the Lord will discipline us, just like he did with David, and provide the appropriate consequences.

Questions to Ponder

▶ When was the last time I was caught in a lie, and how did I handle it?

▶ How do I treat my loyal friends?

▶ What sinful habits do I need to break free from in my life, and how can I stop sins from escalating?

The Truth About Consequences

As our sins multiply, so do the consequences (David).

Chapter 7

WHY AM I INSIDE A WHALE?

During a recent trip to Antarctica with my daughter, we encountered seals, penguins, and whales while cruising around in small inflatable boats. The whales were huge and honestly a bit scary up close, and it would have been easy for one of the large and mighty humpbacks to flip our small rubber boat. I was very thankful we did not end up in the frigid water or inside the belly of one of them, like Jonah.

The Story of Jonah

The Bible does not record many details about Jonah. He is referenced in 2 Kings 14:25 as having lived during the period when the Israelites were divided into two kingdoms, Judah and Israel. Jonah was one of the few prophets from the Northern Kingdom of Israel. During this time, Israel was under the reign of Jeroboam II, one of Israel's many wicked kings. Most scholars credit Jonah with writing the book of the Bible that bears his name, which tells the truthful story of his less than flattering encounter with the Lord.

The kingdom of Israel had many enemies at that time, but the greatest threat was from Assyria, a kingdom that would later invade and conquer Israel. Nineveh was the capital city of Assyria, and today the remains are located near Mosul, Iraq.

Most believers know the story of Jonah and the whale. It is a favorite with kids in Sunday school, as it paints a very graphic image about what happens when we do not listen to God and his direction for our lives. We will dig into this story to grasp just how Jonah ended up inside a whale as a consequence of his actions: "The LORD gave this message to Jonah son of Amittai: 'Get up and go to the great city of Nineveh. Announce my judgment against it because I have seen how wicked its people are'" (Jonah 1:1–2 NLT).

The first thing to notice is Jonah heard directly from the Lord and was given a very specific direction or calling. As a prophet, Jonah had taken the time and effort to develop a relationship with the Lord, so he could clearly hear the voice of God. Next, the Lord gave Jonah a dangerous and daunting task. God told Jonah to travel hundreds of miles, to the capital city of Nineveh in Assyria, which was Israel's greatest enemy at that time. The people of Nineveh knew the Israelites worshiped a single God, but they did not know him, as they worshiped a number of different pagan gods. It was quite a challenging assignment to be directed by God to travel to this hostile city, then proclaim its impending destruction unless the people turned to Israel's God. How many of us would embrace that arduous mission from the Lord?

The most difficult part for Jonah was knowing the Lord was merciful and would forgive the people of Nineveh if they changed their evil ways. Jonah's preference was for God to destroy those wicked people, who he considered his enemies. Jonah had strong personal prejudices against them, and he did not want to see them saved from destruction if they repented from their pagan belief system. Jonah did not embrace God's plan to bring his message to an enemy nation, nor did Jonah show them the blessings God wanted all Israelites to show to other nations. So, even though Jonah was the Lord's prophet and had a specific calling to go to Nineveh to preach God's message, Jonah ran in the opposite direction to Tarshish.

Fleeing to Tarshish was about as far away from Nineveh as Jonah could travel in those days. Nineveh was about seven hundred miles (1,100 kilometers) northeast from where Jonah lived in Gath-Hepher, a small border town near Galilee. However, Jonah traveled in the opposite direction, southwest, down to the port city of Joppa (Tel Aviv today). Then, he booked passage on a ship to Tarshish, which was an additional three thousand miles (4,800 kilometers) west across the Mediterranean Sea, which today is the south coast of Spain, near the Strait of Gibraltar. Jonah was definitely running in the opposite direction of where God called him to and what God called him to do. Jonah took his own path apart from God.

● ● ●

What Was Jonah's Sin?
Running from God and Hating His Enemies

▶▶▶ The Consequences

Then the Lord sent a great wind on the sea, and such a violent storm arose that the ship threatened to break up. All the sailors were afraid and each cried out to his own god. And they threw the cargo into the sea to lighten the ship. But Jonah had gone below deck, where he lay down and fell into a deep sleep. The captain went to him and said, "How can you sleep? Get up and call on your god! Maybe he will take notice of us so that we will not perish." Then the sailors said to each other, "Come, let us cast lots to find out who is responsible for this calamity." They cast lots and the lot fell on Jonah. So they asked him, "Tell us, who is responsible for making all this trouble for us? What kind of work do you do? Where do you come from? What is your country? From what people are you?" He answered, "I am a Hebrew and I worship the Lord, the God of heaven, who made the sea and the dry land." This terrified them and they asked, "What have you done?" (They knew he was running away from the Lord, because he had already told them so.) (Jonah 1:4–10)

We see how Jonah's sin affected the lives of those around him. First, all the cargo had to be thrown overboard, which was a great financial loss to the owners. Then, the captain and crew feared for their lives, as they knew it was not a common storm. When asked, Jonah proclaimed he served the Lord, the God of heaven, but he was a poor example of one of God's prophets when he revealed he was running away. It did not take long for the men on the ship to determine Jonah was the reason for the storm, and something needed to be done before they all perished.

> The sea was getting rougher and rougher. So they asked him, "What should we do to you to make the sea calm down for us?" "Pick me up and throw me into the sea," he replied, "and it will become calm. I know that it is my fault that this great storm has come upon you." Instead, the men did their best to row back to land. But they could not, for the sea grew even wilder than before. Then they cried out to the LORD, "Please, LORD, do not let us die for taking this man's life. Do not hold us accountable for killing an innocent man, for you, LORD, have done as you pleased." Then they took Jonah and threw him overboard, and the raging sea grew calm. At this the men greatly feared the LORD, and they offered a sacrifice to the LORD and made vows to him. (Jonah 1:11–16)

Jonah knew the Lord had brought the storm upon their ship due to his sinful actions, and he accepted responsibility for it. The sailors did their best to save the ship, but Jonah told them to throw him overboard. He did not jump overboard himself, since as a prophet, Jonah knew that suicide was forbidden by Jewish law. As a consequence of his sin, Jonah accepted the anticipated sacrificial death of being thrown into the sea. After asking for forgiveness, the crew threw Jonah into the water, and immediately the wind and waves calmed down. The sailors quickly learned the power of the God of heaven, and followed the Lord from that moment on. Jonah was ready for death, but the Lord had a different plan.

Jonah ended up inside a huge fish, which we will continue to describe as a whale. There are conflicting scientific reports if someone could survive inside the stomach of either a whale or a huge fish for three days.[3] The Lord accomplished many supernatural things throughout the Bible, and I believe this was one of them. Regardless, I cannot image a worse place to be for three days than inside a whale's stomach. First, it had to be completely dark. Next, it smelled terrible due to digestive acids in the stomach, and the acid probably burned Jonah's sin.

● ● ●

The first thing Jonah did was pray. He reflected on his previous actions during that miserable three-day experience inside the whale. We see Jonah recounting the harrowing events in the water, and then he turned his life back to completely surrender to God. He acknowledged his sin and separation from God, and the consequences resulting from his sin. Jonah realized embracing God's plan for his life was better than running away. After three days inside the belly of the fish, Jonah called out in grateful praise to the Lord and the fish vomited him out.

It is awesome to know God commands all the fish in the seas. God had the whale vomit Jonah onto dry land, not an easy task and another miracle in my eyes, so Jonah did not even have to swim to shore. Jonah's consequence taught him he could not run from God. We will cover the rest of the story concerning Nineveh in the next chapter.

How Does This Relate to Me Today?

Have you ever felt as if you were inside a whale, or outside of God's will for your life? What did you do the last time the Lord gave you a difficult task to accomplish? Did you embrace it or run in the opposite direction? How would you react if the Lord asked you to work with people you were uncomfortable with, either in your country or in a foreign land? What does the Lord need to do to get your attention when you are heading in the wrong direction?

The story of Jonah is the perfect example of the importance of listening to God and doing what he tells us to do, and I cannot emphasize that too many times in this book. As we mature in our ability to hear from the Lord, he will guide us into his perfect path for our lives. We always have a choice, though, just like Jonah. Our primary focus should be to listen to God and obey. It is much better to stay close to God, to listen for, and to follow his direction, rather than navigating your own path separately from his will for your life.

Many times in my life I have felt a prompting from the Lord either to do or not do something, but I ignored it or ran the other way like Jonah. Some of those stories are here in this book. If you are not skilled yet at hearing from the Lord, those promptings can come in the form of angst or an unsettled feeling in your spirit or conscience when you are about to do something wrong or make a bad decision. Then, it is your choice whether to follow the Lord and do the right thing or run from God and righteousness.

Once, the Lord gave me a strange command to follow, and he had to yell at me in a very unpleasant manner to get my attention. It was shortly after I moved into one of the busiest senior leadership positions I ever had as a colonel in the military. Regardless of my military workload, I always stayed engaged attending services and classes in a local church wherever I was stationed. My church had just announced its upcoming fall Christian education classes. One option was a six-week class reviewing Joel Osteen's latest book, and the other option was taking classes through Life Christian University, in pursuit of a Bachelor of Arts degree in theology. At first, I was excited to study the Osteen book, but then I started to feel a tugging in my spirit toward the theology degree classes. At that point, I had a Bachelor of Science degree in mechanical engineering and three different Master of Science degrees, so getting another degree did not make sense in my mind. I knew attending the Joel Osteen class would be much easier than all the homework and tests required for the theology degree. Just like Jonah, I wanted to run away from something difficult and tried to substitute something easier in its place.

Being a methodical person, I went out to an empty park on a Sunday afternoon and wrote out a pros and cons list for each option. I knew on paper, it would make sense to do the Joel Osteen class, as I could not fathom the need for another degree. Plus, with my challenging and time-consuming military workload, I could not imagine having the energy to attend night classes as well. As soon as I made the decision to sign up for the Joel Osteen class, I heard someone loudly yell my name. I looked all around the park to see who had called me, but I was still all alone. Then I heard, "You need to get that theology degree for something I have in store for you in the future." Whether I physically heard that voice or it was in my spirit, I cannot confirm, but it was loud. I experienced firsthand the fear of the Lord. I could have run from God and continued to pursue my own agenda. However, quickly and obediently, I signed up for the theology degree classes and spent the next two years in night school. Even though initially I was afraid of the additional school workload, I really enjoyed all of my theology classes and graduated with all As. I did not enjoy being yelled at in that park by God to do something he wanted me to do. From that point on, I learned to pray and listen for God's "still small voice" so he does not have to yell at me to get my attention.

Only God knew how important it was to have a theology degree for my ministry career, and I am so grateful I did not run from it. God also knew I would have the time, energy, and fortitude to complete the degree despite my military workload. That theology degree gave me credibility to teach Christian education classes while I was still in active military service. I taught two different weekly Bible studies at the military chapel during a yearlong deployment to Afghanistan, as well as leading additional Bible studies in my home for many years. Now that I am retired from the military and serving in ministry full time, that degree has opened the door for me to teach at several Bible schools around the world, plus it provided the majority of the needed classes for my minister ordination through the Assemblies of God. My obedience to God in getting that degree has blessed my ministry career much more than I ever thought possible.

If we want to be faithful to God, we need to do everything he asks of us, not just the easy and fun things we want to do. Sometimes, he will ask us to do something we do not understand at the time, but it will become clear later on. The Lord may even ask us to do things just to test us and see if we will be obedient. We cannot run and hide from God, as his Word tells us: "Where can I go from your Spirit? Where can I flee from your presence? If I go up to the heavens, you are there; if I make my bed in the depths, you are there. If I rise on the wings of the dawn, if I settle on the far side of the sea, even there your hand will guide me, your right hand will hold me fast" (Psalm 139:7–10).

Listen, obey, and do whatever God asks of you. Jonah was asked to do something he did not want to do, and he faced consequences when he ran from it. When we do not comply, we are running from God.

Questions to Ponder

▶ In what areas in my life am I running from God right now?

▶ How is my sin affecting the lives of those around me?

▶ Do I model godly behavior in both my words and actions, especially to those who are outside of my culture and faith?

The Truth About Consequences

We can't run from God; he always finds us (Jonah).

Chapter 8

THE BIG TURNAROUND

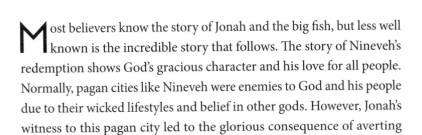

Most believers know the story of Jonah and the big fish, but less well known is the incredible story that follows. The story of Nineveh's redemption shows God's gracious character and his love for all people. Normally, pagan cities like Nineveh were enemies to God and his people due to their wicked lifestyles and belief in other gods. However, Jonah's witness to this pagan city led to the glorious consequence of averting destruction and receiving everlasting life.

Jonah did not like the Assyrian people since they were Israel's enemies. The main reason Jonah ran from God's assignment was his hateful prejudices against the wicked Ninevites, who lived in the capital city of Assyria. Jonah knew the Lord was a loving and forgiving God, but Jonah did not want to see the Ninevites turn from their evil ways to receive life. Jonah felt his enemies should be destroyed.

The people of Nineveh had cause for concern, since God had previously destroyed a similarly wicked city (see Genesis 13:13; 19:24–29). The destruction story of Sodom and Gomorrah was passed down through the generations and written in Israel's historical scrolls, so the story was likely known to the Ninevites.

In chapter 7, we saw Jonah flee in the opposite direction after being given the command to go to Nineveh. That did not turn out well for Jonah, as he was thrown off a ship in the middle of a God-ordained storm. It took three days inside the belly of a whale for Jonah to see the error of his ways and repent. Once Jonah returned to dry land, "then the word of the LORD came to Jonah a second time: 'Go to the great city of Nineveh and proclaim to it the message I give you.' Jonah obeyed the word of the LORD and went to Nineveh" (Jonah 3:1–3).

At the second command from the Lord, Jonah dutifully obeyed. Blessings come when we obey the Lord, not only to ourselves but to others as well. "Now Nineveh was a very large city; it took three days to go through it. Jonah began by going a day's journey into the city, proclaiming, 'Forty more days and Nineveh will be overthrown'" (Jonah 3:3–4).

Nineveh was a huge city for that time period. Jonah may not have liked the Ninevites, but he obeyed God's command and preached of Nineveh's pending destruction. It took several days for Jonah to walk throughout the city, warning the people their city would be overthrown if they did not change their wicked ways. We do not know how the people of Nineveh knew that Jonah was God's prophet. Maybe they heard Jonah's miracle whale story and that added to his credibility. I believe the Holy Spirit gave Jonah the right words to turn the hearts of the people of Nineveh, because when he spoke, something incredible happened:

> The Ninevites believed God. A fast was proclaimed, and all of them, from the greatest to the least, put on sackcloth. When Jonah's warning reached the king of Nineveh, he rose from his throne, took off his royal robes, covered himself with sackcloth and sat down in the dust. This is the proclamation he issued in Nineveh: "By the decree of the king and his nobles: Do not let people or animals, herds or flocks, taste anything; do not let them eat or drink. But let people and animals be covered with sackcloth. Let everyone call urgently on God. Let them give up their evil ways and their violence. Who knows? God may yet relent and with compassion turn from his fierce anger so that we will not perish." (Jonah 3:5–9)

● ● ●

Ninevah's Faith in Action
The People Believed and Repented

The people heard and believed Jonah. First, they put on sackcloth, which was a very uncomfortable garment, especially compared to the normal luxurious clothes they were used to wearing. Next, the people of the city initiated a likely day time fast, which probably lasted the entire forty days.[4] Then, when Jonah's proclamation reached the king of Nineveh, he decreed an official fast which was extended to include animals, and he also humbled himself to sackcloth and dust. It was a total surrender to Israel's God, believing in faith they might still be spared from destruction. Their total commitment and repentance had a profound effect on their lives.

▶▶▶ The Positive Consequences

Back in chapter 5 we saw the rewards of long life and entrance into the Promised Land given to Caleb and Joshua due to their faithfulness and trust in God. It is wonderful to see another example of positive consequences. "When God saw what they did and how they turned from their evil ways, he relented and did not bring on them the destruction he had threatened" (Jonah 3:10). The king and the entire city repented of their sinful and wicked ways and turned to God. Their repentance took them off the path of destruction and gave them everlasting life. This shows God's true heart for all people and nations, as he gives everyone the opportunity to repent, change their wicked ways, and follow him.

● ● ●

The final chapter of Jonah details a sad story concerning Jonah's anger at God for showing grace to Israel's enemies. However, our loving God showed Jonah mercy and explained: "And should I not have concern for the great city of Nineveh, in which there are more than a hundred and twenty thousand people who cannot tell their right hand from their left—and also many animals?" (Jonah 4:11).

It is God's will for all people to come to him and not perish. Even though Jonah was angry that God was willing to forgive the Ninevites, his actions led to 120,000 people, who were previously living in spiritual darkness, coming to know the one true God and being able to spend eternity with him. Jesus validated these events and explained this key act of repentance in the Gospel of Matthew.

> Then some of the Pharisees and teachers of the law said to him, "Teacher, we want to see a sign from you." He answered, "A wicked and adulterous generation asks for a sign! But none will be given it except the sign of the prophet Jonah. For as Jonah was three days and three nights in the belly of a huge fish, so the Son of Man will be three days and three nights in the heart of the earth. The men of Nineveh will stand up at the judgment with this generation and condemn it; for they repented at the preaching of Jonah, and now something greater than Jonah is here." (Matthew 12:38–41)

First, Jonah's experience in the big fish was validated by Jesus. Then, Jesus prophesied his own death and the "three days and three nights" to be spent in the tomb before he would be resurrected. Jesus also pointed out that those who fully repented at Nineveh had the authority to condemn those who did not follow him. The people in Nineveh repented and changed from their wicked ways; however, the religious leaders and most of the Jews in Jesus's day did not repent or come to believe in and follow him.

How Does This Relate to Me Today?

Most of us have stories of walking in darkness with Satan, and then seeing the light and following Jesus Christ. It is a free will choice for all people to follow Jesus, though it is difficult for many to commit to following him without guidance from other believers to show them the way to everlasting life. For me, I did not make that decision with my own insight. I knew something was missing, that there was a hole in my spiritual life that needed to be filled. It took a yearlong effort from a work colleague early in my military career to help me become self-aware enough to realize my sinful ways and my need to surrender my life to Jesus Christ. I am blessed the Lord sent that individual, who needed a lot of tenacity and perseverance to get me to see the truth in God's Word and follow Jesus.

Take a minute and think about your own salvation story. Who guided you, and how willing are you to reach out to others in pursuit of their eternity, in either heaven or hell? Will you accept the drama that goes along with talking about Jesus to your family and friends? Like Jonah, how many of you would rather run away than confront your enemies with the gospel? Do you have hidden (or even blatant) prejudices against certain people? Do you hide such anger for your enemies in your heart, that you are OK with them spending eternity in hell? That is not God's way, as it is written, "The Lord . . . does not want anyone to be destroyed, but wants everyone to repent" (2 Peter 3:9 NLT). In addition, Jesus often spoke in the Gospels of how we should treat our enemies. Jesus said, "You have heard that it was said, 'Love your neighbor and hate your enemy.' But I tell you, love your enemies and pray for those who persecute you" (Matthew 5:43–44). We are commanded to love and pray for our enemies.

God taught me an important lesson on how to see the humanity in those I call my enemies, to love them, and to pray for those I fear. My career in the US Air Force involved working through Operation Desert Storm in 1990 and the 9/11 attacks. Secondary to my military training and my own emotional reactions to the tragic events around which I worked so closely, I began to develop a discomfort and regrettably a distrust of individuals from the Middle East and, by extension, Muslims. For my entire career, "the enemies" we were fighting against happened to be predominantly from this area and were practitioners of Islam.

Just a few years after 9/11, it was my turn to go on a deployment to the Middle East. I was going to live on a foreign military base in the United Arab Emirates (UAE), in an area where many local people did not trust Americans, or Christians. Initially, I felt the same lack of trust toward them, but that did not make either of us right. When I arrived in the UAE, I realized how unique the Emirati people were; they looked, acted, and lived so differently than everyone in America, or any other region in the world I had ever been. I did not know anything about Islam, nor did I understand why they dressed so strangely, with the men wearing *kanduras*, or long white dresses, and the women completely covered from head to toe in black garments called *abayas*.

I had an important position, commanding the Expeditionary Mission Support Group, and I was known as the "base" commander for all United States military personnel on the Emirati Al Dhafra Air Base. Right after I took command, I was told that since I was a woman, I would have little to no contact with any of my Emirati male counterparts. I was told that in their culture, such interactions could be seen as inappropriate. Additionally, the locals were unfamiliar with the idea of a female in a leadership role. This innuendo, of course, only fueled my feelings of distrust and dislike.

While touring the ongoing construction throughout the base, an Emirati man, in one of those long white dresses, approached my male military companion about a problem he was having within the US section of the Emirati military base. My companion introduced me to Omar and told him, as the base commander, I could address his concerns. Omar told me about the multiple issues he was having moving his construction materials around the US section of the military base. By making a few calls, I was able to quickly resolve his issues. After that, he nodded approval of my *wasta*, or ability to get things done, and invited me to have coffee in his office. I always had a male military officer join us during our meetings, per local custom. Our chance meeting was really a conducive connection for both of us, and I soon found out that he was the primary Emirati contractor I needed to work with throughout my remaining six-month deployment.

Omar and I began to work together on a number of significant issues and solved many communication problems between the US military and Emirati base leadership. Most importantly, we became friends. We looked different, dressed differently, were raised differently, but found things we had in common, especially our children. Through our friendship, he elucidated many aspects of Islam that I did not understand, and I was able to share my Christian faith with him and explain our belief in Jesus and the Bible's teachings. Omar told me that being a Muslim is a way of life in the UAE, so converting to Christianity is often problematic, both socially and professionally, for Muslims. However, by being open and friendly with someone so different than myself, I was able to show him the love of Christ.

Even today, when I hear stories of evil acts attributed to Muslims, I measure everything in terms of my friend Omar, since he was a good and honorable man. As soon as I returned home from the deployment, I took a wonderful class called "Encountering the World of Islam" so I would have a greater understanding of the tenets of Islam and be better equipped for future discussions with Muslims. I have learned that whether a person commits good or horrible deeds, prejudices or judgment based on ethnicity or religion have no place. I have since taken several more classes on understanding the history of Islam, which has helped me in the Muslim nations where I serve today. I now have a heart for and pray for all Muslims, and hope they will come to know Jesus as their loving Savior, the only path to God. I also continue to pray for my friend Omar and believe the seeds I planted in him will lead to his everlasting life.

Who are you willing to talk to about Jesus? Are you brave enough to discuss faith with your family and friends, or go a step further and share Jesus's love with your "enemies"? How far are you willing to go to take a stand for Christ? Paul told us to "do the work of an evangelist" (2 Timothy 4:5). Peter said we should "worship Christ as Lord of your life. And if someone asks about your hope as a believer, always be ready to explain it. But do this in a gentle and respectful way. Keep your conscience clear. Then if people speak against you, they will be ashamed when they see what a good life you live because you belong to Christ" (1 Peter 3:15–16 NLT).

God always wants us to be a light for him and to share the love of Jesus in the dark places of this world, especially where evil runs rampant. How willing are you to share the gospel in a foreign country? Or financially support others to go? Are you willing to take classes on other faiths, so you can learn their backgrounds in order to better bring the gospel of Christ to them? Are your own attitudes and prejudices part of the problem, and something you need to work on to become more accepting of others? Looking inward, critiquing, and then fixing our own bad attitudes is never easy, but it may be required for the work the Lord has called you to do.

What about showing the love of Christ closer to home? Are you willing to serve and help support a local organization that supports homelessness, addiction, prison ministry, or refugees? Here is something even simpler: inviting a friend, coworker, or neighbor to church. How is the Lord convicting you in these areas? All these activities may seem scary, but remember the Lord is always with you, and he will guide you in your words and actions. You cannot, and should not, try to force people to believe in Jesus, as it is a free will choice. However, by stepping out in faith, serving others, and sharing how Jesus rescued you, you, too, could turn around a person, a family, or maybe even a city like Jonah did. Jesus told us, "There is rejoicing in the presence of the angels of God over one sinner who repents" (Luke 15:10).

Just like Jonah, you can be the facilitator of such positive consequences as felt by the Ninevites by being a Christian leader, teacher, evangelist, or just a good example. When you show those who do not know Jesus how to believe and confess with true repentance in their hearts, it will reverse the destruction in their lives, and they will receive everlasting life with Jesus Christ.

Questions to Ponder

▶ How can I be braver and more outgoing to share the gospel of Jesus Christ with my family, friends, and coworkers?

▶ How can I become more comfortable around people who are different from me?

▶ How can I take the initiative to understand the struggles of those of different races, religions, and socioeconomic classes so that I may find common ground with them and reach out to them with the love of Jesus Christ?

The Truth About Consequences

True repentance can turn destruction into everlasting life (Nineveh's Redemption).

Chapter 9

IS IT OK TO TELL A LITTLE WHITE LIE?

Our next short but powerful biblical story is from the New Testament and can be a difficult one for many people to understand. How could a "small" lie result in such a "big" consequence? As you read this story, think about the three following questions: What were Ananias and Sapphira's motives for giving? What did the Holy Spirit reveal about their true character? How much time did they have to repent of their sin? We will start with an overview of the early church that Ananias and Sapphira were a part of at that time.

The Story of the Early Church

The Gospels of Matthew, Mark, Luke, and John tell the awe-inspiring story of Jesus's life and ministry, including the persecution he and his followers endured. Jesus did not follow the strict Jewish traditions of the time, and it upset the Jewish religious leaders. Jesus knew that there was corruption in the synagogue and that many religious leaders of that time cared more about their high social standing than the people they were supposed to serve. Jesus told the Pharisees, "You like to appear righteous in public, but God knows your hearts. What this world honors is detestable in the sight of God" (Luke 16:15 NLT). Jesus's teachings were very different from those found in Jewish law at that time. The idea that God preferred love for others instead of vengeance and forgiveness over punishment was radical at that time.

The persecution of Jesus's followers continued after his death and resurrection, and much of it is recorded in the book of Acts. Several miracles performed by the remaining disciples resulted in huge growth in the body of believers, and this group became the first Christian church, called the "Way." These believers in Jesus Christ came together as a church community, with harmony throughout the group and an abundance of sharing.

> All the believers were united in heart and mind. And they felt that what they owned was not their own, so they shared everything they had. The apostles testified powerfully to the resurrection of the Lord Jesus, and God's great blessing was upon them all. There were no needy people among them, because those who owned land or houses would sell them and bring the money to the apostles to give to those in need. (Acts 4:32–35 NLT)

These acts of sharing and love were completely voluntary, as there was no mandate from Peter or any of the other leaders to provide financial support for the church at that time. It was the Holy Spirit who encouraged these believers to support each other in love and to give whatever amount they wanted. The Bible records a specific example: "For instance, there was Joseph, the one the apostles nicknamed Barnabas (which means "Son of Encouragement"). He was from the tribe of Levi and came from the island of Cyprus. He sold a field he owned and brought the money to the apostles" (Acts 4:36–37 NLT).

The Bible tells us much more about Barnabas throughout the book of Acts, as he became one of the apostle Paul's traveling companions. The Bible does not record if individuals like Barnabas, who gave so unselfishly, received a great deal of praise and adoration from the church and its leaders. We can assume that happened, as the Bible verses that immediately follow describe a sinful action by two others in the church body who were seeking that kind of recognition.

Ananias and Sapphira

After the Bible mentions the righteous acts of charity by Barnabas, it takes us right to the story of Ananias and Sapphira. *Ananias* means "God is gracious," and *Sapphira* means "beautiful"; however, we will find out that these names did not reflect their true natures. "But there was a certain man named Ananias who, with his wife, Sapphira, sold some property. He brought part of the money to the apostles, claiming it was the full amount. With his wife's consent, he kept the rest" (Acts 5:1–2 NLT).

Most scholars agree that since Ananias and Sapphira were part of the church body, they were also believers in Jesus Christ. Despite that, believers can be tempted by Satan to sin. This husband and wife appear to present a similar, generous financial gift to the church, like Barnabas, by selling some of their property and presenting the funds to the body of believers. The couple, however, was envious of the recognition righteous donors had gained in the community.[5] Sadly, Ananias and Sapphira lied and told the apostles the amount they presented was the entire amount of the sale of their property. They acted with hypocrisy, which "was a deliberate deception, trying to make people think they were more spiritual than they really were."[6]

Of course, it is not a sin to manage your own finances or to sell an asset and keep the money for future investments. The sins in this case, besides lying, were Ananias and Sapphira's envy of Barnabas, and the hypocrisy of using a supposed act of generosity to disguise their own sinful ulterior motives for undo recognition. There was also an element of greed, by keeping back some of the money and not trusting in God to care for all their needs. This story is similar to the story in Joshua 7, when a man named Achan greedily kept some of the spoils of war for himself, and the Lord took judgment on him and his entire family.[7]

• • •

What Were Ananias and Sapphira's Sins?

Lying, Envy, Hypocrisy, and Greed

The Holy Spirit revealed this deception to Peter, who was leading the church at that time. "Then Peter said, 'Ananias, why have you let Satan fill your heart? You lied to the Holy Spirit, and you kept some of the money for yourself. The property was yours to sell or not sell, as you wished. And after selling it, the money was also yours to give away. How could you do a thing like this? You weren't lying to us but to God!'" (Acts 5:3–4 NLT).

Peter told Ananias that the truth would have been better and would have been just as accepted from the church body. Obviously, Ananias wanted that same credit and praise as Barnabas and the other generous givers. Ananias's motives were not right, and we will see firsthand that no one can hide their motives and sins from God.

Peter highlighted how Ananias allowed Satan to lead him astray, as sin is always a choice. Satan continually tempts all believers. Most churches are aware of Satan's attacks from outside the church, and those are easy to guard against. However, Satan diligently tries to tempt us with destructive situations in church as well, and these temptations can be the most difficult to identify, and especially devastating in the end.

The Consequences

The consequence from Ananias's sins was immediate. "As soon as Ananias heard these words, he fell to the floor and died. Everyone who heard about it was terrified. Then some young men got up, wrapped him in a sheet, and took him out and buried him" (Acts 5:5–6 NLT).

Ananias instantly dropped dead. He was not given any time to ponder his sin or the opportunity to confess and repent. Word of his hypocrisy and resulting punishment spread quickly throughout the church. Would his wife fare any better?

About three hours later his wife came in, not knowing what had happened. Peter asked her, "Was this the price you and your husband received for your land?" "Yes," she replied, "that was the price." And Peter said, "How could the two of you even think of conspiring to test the Spirit of the Lord like this? The young men who buried your husband are just outside the door, and they will carry you out, too." Instantly, she fell to the floor and died. When the young men came in and saw that she was dead, they carried her out and buried her beside her husband. Great fear gripped the entire church and everyone else who heard what had happened. (Acts 5:7–11 NLT)

Sapphira was given a chance to recant her story, yet she sustained the lie and immediately died just like her husband.

● ● ●

In God's perspective, they were pretending to be holier than they were. If they had just told Peter the truth—that they were giving only a portion of the money they received—they would have been fine. However, both Ananias and Sapphira wanted the church leaders and body to think they were truly holy and full of righteousness for performing such a generous act. Instead, it was an act full of hypocrisy and greed.

There is some debate about whether Ananias and Sapphira are in heaven or hell. I believe they are in heaven, since they were believers in Jesus Christ, but they lost some of the heavenly rewards they would have received. By dying so quickly, they were not able to advance the kingdom of God like they could have, and therefore did not receive any rewards for continuing the work to promote the gospel of Jesus Christ.

The fear of the Lord came upon the entire community after this incident. It was clear that God expected his people to *truly* be holy and righteous and not to give in to Satan and his material temptations. Believers cannot lie, cheat, or pretend with the church or other believers without consequences. This event was necessary to safeguard the church's purity for its upcoming growth.[8]

How Does This Relate to Me Today?

The tough lessons we learned from Ananias and Sapphira highlight some areas we need to think about in our own lives. First, what is our true motivation for giving to the Lord? We need to realize there are over two thousand verses in the Bible concerning money, so it is an important principle to God. Giving to God must come first, and there are two distinct formats. *Tithing* is returning 10 percent of what God has given us in our income, in the form of giving to our local church. *Offerings* are financial gifts, in addition to the tithe, that provide funds for additional church projects, or to support missions or ministries apart from our local church. There are several good books on the market if you are interested in more details concerning our responsibilities to give back to God what he first gave us.

I want to highlight a couple of key principles related to financial giving that Jesus mentioned. He said, "It is more blessed to give than to receive" (Acts 20:35). As I grow older, I take more joy in giving gifts to my daughter and friends than I do in receiving gifts. I do not need any more "stuff." Jesus also showed us he knows if we are giving out of our abundance or as a sacrifice: "While Jesus was in the Temple, he watched the rich people dropping their gifts in the collection box. Then a poor widow came by and dropped in two small coins. 'I tell you the truth,' Jesus said, 'this poor widow has given more than all the rest of them. For they have given a tiny part of their surplus, but she, poor as she is, has given everything she has'" (Luke 21:1–4 NLT).

Jesus also taught us about the attitude we should have toward giving, which Ananias and Sapphira did not follow.

> Watch out! Don't do your good deeds publicly, to be admired by others, for you will lose the reward from your Father in heaven. When you give to someone in need, don't do as the hypocrites

do—blowing trumpets in the synagogues and streets to call attention to their acts of charity! I tell you the truth, they have received all the reward they will ever get. But when you give to someone in need, don't let your left hand know what your right hand is doing. Give your gifts in private, and your Father, who sees everything, will reward you. (Matthew 6:1–4 NLT)

Some believers have the spiritual gift of giving, and they receive great joy in doing it. For the rest of us, this is an attitude we must learn to develop. Go to the Lord and ask him when and how much to give, whenever you are asked. There is an element of trust involved for both the giver and the receiver of a gift. Those who give should realize the Lord will honor the gifts and bless the giver in return for their financial (or other equivalent) gifts. The receiver needs to trust the Lord will provide the finances for the work he called them to do. My ministry relies 100 percent on donations from others, and the Lord always brings in exactly what the ministry needs, in his perfect timing.

When God calls you to give an offering to a particular ministry, do it with a cheerful heart, knowing you are blessing others and the Lord will bless you in return. Look at what Paul said about giving: "You must each decide in your heart how much to give. And don't give reluctantly or in response to pressure. 'For God loves a person who gives cheerfully'" (2 Corinthians 9:7 NLT). Are you giving with a true heart and righteous motives or to be a big shot in your church or community? Make sure you examine your true motives for giving, and determine if you are doing it in line with God's Word.

Another area to consider is how long we can hide our sin. We need to realize that none of us can hide our sin, or get away with it for very long. Jesus said, "For all that is secret will eventually be brought into the open, and everything that is concealed will be brought to light and made known to all" (Luke 8:17 NLT). This becomes more apparent for those serving God in ministry. We all have been witness to the public exposure of prominent Christian leaders whose sin was revealed publicly and, as a result, they instantly lost their positions and sphere of influence. This always paints the church in a negative light. I have followed many Christian leaders and, unfortunately, watched several of them fall in a very significant manner. Bottom line, they sinned, continued to sin, and God allowed their sin to be exposed publicly. They were in high positions of power, so they had a long way to fall. In my experience, the higher your position, the more accountable you are and the farther you have to fall. Many, like myself, who looked to these leaders for spiritual guidance were negatively impacted, and many believers lost trust and faith in the church because of them.

One of them was my pastor in Colorado Springs, Colorado. His fall really shook me and almost impacted my walk of faith. A sad fact is I remember this pastor telling our congregation many times, "There is no such thing as a secret." Yet, even though he knew it and preached it, his secret sin was divulged in a very public way. I bitterly witnessed many believers walk away from our church due to this incident. This pastor also preached, "You will never know what impact your sin will have on others." I did not really understand that statement until I saw it play out concerning his sin.

Several months later, I was attending a conference in the Upper Peninsula of Michigan and heard a local radio talk show criticizing this pastor for his sins. It grieved my spirit to hear such negative talk about a fallen pastor and the sad state of Christian leadership on the radio, in a location almost 1,500 miles away from Colorado Springs. This pastor's mistake and sin had far-reaching national impact, as these types of incidents have made the entire church body look like hypocrites to unbelievers.

One of Satan's biggest goals is to tempt and get Christian leaders to fall, as it disgraces the church in a very public way. We have seen this play out in all Christian denominations, including in the Catholic Church, as rarely a month goes by without a news headline about another impropriety that has come to light.

Back in chapter 1, we examined how God knows the motives of our heart. God also know our secrets. Look what is written in Hebrews: "Nothing in all creation is hidden from God. Everything is naked and exposed before his eyes, and he is the one to whom we are accountable" (Hebrews 4:13 NLT).

The good news is the Bible gives us instructions. Look what Paul wrote:

> For once you were full of darkness, but now you have light from the Lord. So live as people of light! For this light within you produces only what is good and right and true. Carefully determine what pleases the Lord. Take no part in the worthless deeds of evil and darkness; instead, expose them. It is shameful even to talk about the things that ungodly people do in secret. But their evil intentions will be exposed when the light shines on them, for the light makes everything visible. (Ephesians 5:8–14 NLT)

We cannot hide our sins in the darkness of this world because the Lord sees all. The Bible gives us sound advice on how to walk in faith: "Therefore, since through God's mercy we have this ministry, we do not lose heart. Rather, we have renounced secret and shameful ways; we do not use deception, nor do we distort the word of God. On the contrary, by setting forth the truth plainly we commend ourselves to everyone's conscience in the sight of God" (2 Corinthians 4:1–2).

This reminds us to walk in the Truth of Jesus Christ and the Word of God. Remember, we will be judged by Jesus for not only our walk of faith but our secrets as well: "And this is the message I proclaim—that the day is coming when God, through Christ Jesus, will judge everyone's secret life" (Romans 2:16 NLT). We cannot hide our sins or motives from God. If we do not correct our behavior, repent, and stop our sinful ways, then we too may experience a very severe, and likely public, correction.

A final question we need to think about is how much time we have to confess our sins and repent before we die. None of us knows how much time we have left on this earth. Your life could end very soon, just after you read this sentence, or not for another ten, fifty, or eighty years. There are too many people who think they will have time later to make their lives right with God. Are you so busy with day-to-day life that you do not take time to be with God, praying or reading his Word? Do you think you can just wait until you are older to attend church, read the Bible, pray, and confess your sins? The story of Ananias and Sapphira's quick deaths should be a strong motivator for you to realize you should not wait another minute. If you have sins in your past, confess them now. If you commit a sin later today, confess it immediately. You cannot count on having time for a deathbed confession of your sins when your time comes. So, renounce your secrets, confess your sins immediately, and start and end every day in the right place with God.

We have no secrets in our lives. The Lord knows our motives in terms of giving and all the sins we commit. We should do our best to live a life of righteousness, which is an attribute of our holy and perfect Father God. *Righteousness* is defined as having the same character, faithfulness, and nature of God. It is striving to be right in the eyes of God, including our character, conscience or attitude, and our conduct.[9] Jesus told us to "seek the Kingdom of God above all else, and live righteously, and he will give you everything you need" (Matthew 6:33 NLT). Remember, God knows what is truly in your heart, focus on being righteous, get your spiritual life right with God *now*, and stay that way.

Questions to Ponder

▶ When I give to the Lord, am I just giving out of my excess? Was there a time I gave even though I was on shaky financial footing myself?

▶ Was there a time I did an action "in the name of the Lord" but had an ulterior motive for personal gain?

▶ Am I ready to face God if I die in this minute?

The Truth About Consequences

God knows your true motives, so continually strive for righteousness because consequences can be immediate (Ananias and Sapphira).

Chapter 10

HOW CAN I ENDURE MY CONSEQUENCES?

S ince you have made it this far into the book, I am sure you have
identified some of the consequences from your past. You may think
back in joy at the positive consequences from your acts of faithfulness
and obedience to God. However, you may be concerned about the negative consequences you are still suffering from your past sins, so this
chapter will focus on those consequences.

It may not seem fair that we continue to endure negative consequences, since God forgives our sins when we confess and repent.
However, consequences are the result of past actions, and we have seen
many examples so far of strong believers in the Bible who had lasting
negative consequences due to their sins. If you are like me, you may
find some of these consequences very challenging, and you may be
feeling the heavy weight of them. How can we bear the weight of the
consequences due to our sinful actions? Can any good come from our
negative consequences?

The apostle Paul gave us hope in this area, as few individuals suffered
more than he did. Paul was a key biblical figure. He was a central character in the book of Acts and wrote more books in the New Testament than
any other author. Above all, regardless of his struggles, Paul continued

proclaiming the gospel of Jesus Christ for decades. Before Paul started his ministry serving Jesus, his name was Saul, and he committed many violent acts against the followers of Jesus Christ.

Saul's Background

Saul, a highly educated Pharisee, lived during the same time period as Jesus and had a very high standing among Jewish leaders. Saul wrote that he was "born in Tarsus of Cilicia, but brought up in this city [Jerusalem]. I studied under Gamaliel and was thoroughly trained in the law of our ancestors. I was just as zealous for God as any of you are today" (Acts 22:3). Gamaliel was the top Jewish scholar and most honored rabbi of that time, and being his student gave Saul impressive Jewish credentials.

Since Saul was from Tarsus, he had extensive knowledge of both the Roman and Greek languages and cultures, as Tarsus was a key Roman trade route on the Mediterranean Sea. Tarsus is still located on the south central coast of Turkey, just north of the island of Cyprus. Saul had skill as a tentmaker, which allowed him to support himself as he traveled. He also had the unique benefit of being "born a [Roman] citizen" (Acts 22:28), which granted him many rights that were not available to a typical Hebrew at that time.

Saul spoke of his prestigious Jewish heritage: "circumcised on the eighth day, of the people of Israel, of the tribe of Benjamin, a Hebrew of Hebrews; in regard to the law, a Pharisee; as for zeal, persecuting the church; as for righteousness based on the law, faultless" (Philippians 3:5–6). In addition, he had a family legacy as "a Pharisee, descended from Pharisees" (Acts 23:6). It was easy for Saul to be a young man full of pride, but that would soon change.

We Meet Saul

No reference exists in the Bible that Saul ever saw or heard Jesus speak before his death, resurrection, and ascension into heaven. The story of Saul begins with him overseeing and approving the first killing of a member of the early church for the crime of blasphemy. Stephen, one of the early church leaders, condemned the Jewish religious leaders for their ill treatment of Jesus Christ and the previous prophets sent by God. The Jewish leaders considered Stephen's comments as blasphemous. They "dragged him out of the city and began to stone him. His accusers took off their coats and laid them at the feet of a young man named Saul. . . . Saul was one of the witnesses, and he agreed completely with the killing of Stephen" (Acts 7:58; 8:1 NLT).

The killing of Stephen started "a great wave of persecution . . . sweeping over the church in Jerusalem; and all the believers except the apostles were scattered through the regions of Judea and Samaria" (Acts 8:1 NLT). The scattering of the church seemed bad at first, but it succeeded in spreading the good news of Jesus Christ throughout the region. Saul was the leader in the persecution of the early church. He was zealous to keep the Jewish way of life and did everything he could to stop the spread of the gospel. Saul went "everywhere to destroy the church. He went from house to house, dragging out both men and women to throw them into prison" (Acts 8:3 NLT).

When Saul realized many believers were scattered and many had relocated up to Damascus, Saul decided to go there as well. "Saul was uttering threats with every breath and was eager to kill the Lord's followers. So he went to the high priest. He requested letters addressed to the synagogues in Damascus, asking for their cooperation in the arrest of any followers of the Way he found there. He wanted to bring them—both men and women—back to Jerusalem in chains" (Acts 9:1–2 NLT).

In his own words, Saul said, "I persecuted the followers of this Way to their death, arresting both men and women and throwing them into prison, as the high priest and all the Council can themselves testify. I even obtained letters from them to their associates in Damascus, and went there to bring these people as prisoners to Jerusalem to be punished" (Acts 22:4–5).

What Was Saul's Sin?

By persecuting Jesus Christ's followers, Saul was persecuting Jesus

Christ. It took a dramatic experience for Saul to turn away from his zealous persecution of believers.

> As [Saul] was approaching Damascus on this mission, a light from heaven suddenly shone down around him. He fell to the ground and heard a voice saying to him, "Saul! Saul! Why are you persecuting me?" "Who are you, lord?" Saul asked. And the voice replied, "I am Jesus, the one you are persecuting! Now get up and go into the city, and you will be told what you must do." The men with Saul stood speechless, for they heard the sound of someone's voice but saw no one! Saul picked himself up off the ground, but when he opened his eyes he was blind. So his companions led him by the hand to Damascus. He remained there blind for three days and did not eat or drink. (Acts 9:3–9 NLT)

Saul met Jesus face-to-face and was confronted for his sins. Then, he had three days to ponder what had happened to him. To help Saul understand the Lord's expectations, God sent Ananias (a different Ananias than in the last chapter), a disciple of Jesus living in that region: "Now there was a believer in Damascus named Ananias. The Lord spoke to him in a vision, calling, 'Ananias!' 'Yes, Lord!' he replied. . . . The Lord said, 'Go, for Saul is my chosen instrument to take my message to the Gentiles and to kings, as well as to the people of Israel. And I will show him how much he must suffer for my name's sake'" (Acts 9:10, 15–16 NLT).

After Saul received his sight back, he confessed his sins, repented, received the Holy Spirit, and was baptized. He spent many days in Damascus with other followers of Jesus, and then immediately started preaching in the synagogues that Jesus was the Son of God. This started Saul's own experience with persecution, as he had to leave Damascus in the dead of night to escape a plot by the Jewish religious leaders to kill him. Saul was targeted by Jewish religious leaders and even believers for many years.

The Jewish religious leaders were outraged that Saul converted from his Jewish faith to believe that Jesus was the long-awaited Messiah. In addition, most of Jesus's followers were still afraid of Saul and did not trust his conversion, so he could not remain in Jerusalem. Once Saul started his missionary work to both Greek and Roman Gentiles, he used the name Paul, which was his Roman name. Interestingly, Paul had many unique qualities that made him the perfect missionary to travel throughout the Roman and Greek territories to spread the gospel. He was fluent in the Greek language and culture, could support himself through tent-making, and had the privileges of being a Roman citizen.

Paul had been cruel to many followers of Jesus, but he turned his life around to follow Jesus Christ. He acknowledged his sins, proclaimed what he gained through his conversion, and highlighted the calling he was given by the Lord to preach to the Gentiles.

Did Paul Suffer Consequences?

The Bible does not come right out and say that Paul suffered consequences for his former actions. However, he did not have an easy life following his conversion. He faced challenges from the remaining disciples as they had concerns over his true conversion. He faced persecution from both the Jewish religious leaders and pagan believers just about everywhere he went. Paul also spent many years both in prison cells and under house arrest. Remember this verse: "And I [the Lord] will show [Paul] how much he must suffer for my name's sake" (Acts 9:16 NLT)? Look at Paul's own words:

> I have worked much harder, been in prison more frequently, been flogged more severely, and been exposed to death again and again. Five times I received from the Jews the forty lashes minus one. Three times I was beaten with rods, once I was pelted with stones, three times I was shipwrecked, I spent a night and a day in the open sea, I have been constantly on the move. I have been in danger from rivers, in danger from bandits, in danger from my fellow Jews, in danger from Gentiles; in danger in the

city, in danger in the country, in danger at sea; and in danger from false believers. I have labored and toiled and have often gone without sleep; I have known hunger and thirst and have often gone without food; I have been cold and naked. Besides everything else, I face daily the pressure of my concern for all the churches. (2 Corinthians 11:23–28)

That is a long list of hardships. Were any of those difficulties direct consequences for his sins? Paul inflected a great deal of suffering on the followers of Christ, so, I believe his suffering for Christ came as a consequence for his previous actions of persecuting believers. I am led to think Paul believed that as well, due to his diligence to spread the gospel of Christ throughout the rest of his life.

Not only did Paul suffer many hardships and trials, but the Lord kept him humble despite his rich spiritual gifts. Paul had great prophetic abilities, plus he was greatly admired and followed for his teaching. You will see here the Lord found a way to keep him humble in the midst of that:

Therefore, in order to keep me from becoming conceited, I was given a thorn in my flesh, a messenger of Satan, to torment me. Three times I pleaded with the Lord to take it away from me. But he said to me, "My grace is sufficient for you, for my power is made perfect in weakness." Therefore I will boast all the more gladly about my weaknesses, so that Christ's power may rest on me. That is why, for Christ's sake, I delight in weaknesses, in insults, in hardships, in persecutions, in difficulties. For when I am weak, then I am strong. (2 Corinthians 12:7–10)

Paul highlighted that even though we may be weak in certain areas of our lives, we are made strong through Christ Jesus. I believe Paul knew and experienced God's grace, and that is what strengthened him during his times of trouble and persecution. Paul knew he did not need to rely on his own abilities, but he could trust in God for all things, at all times, and in all situations.

How Does This Relate to Me Today?

When we look at Paul, we see a story of a man who, when confronted by Jesus, completely turned his life around. Paul had a choice to make after his experience on the road to Damascus. He could have kept the easy life as a Pharisee and continued his pursuit of Jesus's followers, but instead, he chose to follow Jesus completely and embrace the mission and calling that God had given him. Paul had to endure dreadful, life-threatening experiences and trials to continue this calling from God, yet he survived them all. It was during these difficult circumstances that Paul performed many miracles and wrote some of his greatest letters, which are the cornerstone of the New Testament.

I had to learn this tough lesson of fully following and trusting in Jesus during consequences and trials in my own life. In 1986, I gave my life to Christ, and I was a zealous believer for a while. However, I eventually fell into a lukewarm existence of following the Lord, which did not happen overnight. It started when the military moved me overseas, and I lost the support of a strong Bible-believing church and a community of fellow believers to hold me accountable. I still attended church at the military chapel, and I still prayed in tongues, but I was soon living for myself and not walking with Jesus.

How does the Lord feel about lukewarm believers? "I know your deeds, that you are neither cold nor hot. I wish you were either one or the other! So, because you are lukewarm—neither hot nor cold—I am about to spit you out of my mouth. You say, 'I am rich; I have acquired wealth and do not need a thing.' But you do not realize that you are wretched, pitiful, poor, blind and naked" (Revelation 3:15–17). Based on those biblical words, the Lord was not pleased with my lukewarm existence, which stretched on for over fifteen years.

The Bible enforces both discipline and hope in the following verses: "Those whom I love I rebuke and discipline. So be earnest and repent. Here I am! I stand at the door and knock. If anyone hears my voice and opens the door, I will come in and eat with that person, and they with me" (Revelation 3:19–20). The Lord loves us and wants us to walk a righteous path. When we sin, the Lord tells us we will face discipline to correct the sinful behavior, but he also provides directions for us to follow to live a more righteous life. When we sin, it opens the door for the enemy to come in and wreak havoc on our lives. Yet, when we repent and seek God, he draws us in.

Did I face discipline and consequences from my lukewarm and sinful existence? Yes. Within a very short time period in the early 2000s, I went through the most difficult period in my life. Every area of my life came under attack from the enemy all at once: my marriage, family, work, finances, and even my health began to experience setbacks, and I felt like Job in the Old Testament. The hardest ordeal was having to move across the country from my nine-year-old daughter. I tried to separate from the military, just three years short of a military retirement, but since I was in a critical career field and it was shortly after 9/11, I was not allowed to leave the military and was forced to move.

Then, my husband returned from a deployment in Afghanistan where he traumatically witnessed four members of his Special Forces team get killed during a mission, and he struggled with deep feelings of depression and guilt. Soon after his return, I caught him having an affair with a twenty-two-year-old married woman, and our marriage quickly ended. On top of that, even though the military had moved me, I faced a huge career disappointment as I was denied a key position I had worked very hard to attain. It was also during this period that I unexpectedly fell into great debt after unsound financial investments, and then had some medical conditions that required a difficult surgery and long recovery that I had to work through all on my own. Were some, or all, of these consequences from the sins that occurred during my lukewarm existence? I believe so.

Facing so many extreme stressors in my life, I, too, had some choices. I could run to worldly pursuits in an attempt to drown my sorrows, or turn my life around like Paul and make a true commitment to God. I knew it was time to stop my lukewarm existence, get on my knees, and focus 100 percent on God. I had to learn to accept God's grace and let him heal me of my troubles by walking with him daily. This verse was key in my transition: "[God] gives grace generously. As the Scriptures say, 'God opposes the proud but gives grace to the humble.' So humble yourselves before God. Resist the devil, and he will flee from you. Come close to God, and God will come close to you" (James 4:6–8 NLT).

I knew I needed dedicated time with the Lord to understand his grace and come close to him, but like everyone, I was super busy. So, I prayed, *God, if you want me to spend ten minutes tomorrow morning reading the Bible, then wake me up ten minutes before my alarm clock.* The Lord did that every morning over the next week. Then, after feeling the joy of spending several minutes with the Lord every morning, I kept expanding that time so I had more opportunity to commune with God. Those morning fellowships with the Lord really set up my day and helped me to keep my focus on him, following his guidance as I lived through the consequences of my past actions. I still spend the first part of every morning reading, praying, and fellowshiping with God. It has kept me close to him all the years since.

It was during that difficult time that God's response to Paul really made sense to me: "My grace is sufficient for you, for my power is made perfect in weakness" (2 Corinthians 12:9). I learned I can pray to receive God's power during my weakness, and God will give me the strength and grace to face my consequences and trials head-on. It was by descending to my lowest point in life that I learned to rely on God alone, not my own abilities.

We all are enduring consequences and trials, but they are not the same thing. I believe every negative consequence can be considered a trial, as it is a time of suffering. However, not every trial is a consequence of a past sin. It can be difficult to live as a Christian, and despite our best efforts to live a holy life, obstacles and challenges will always be present for us to overcome, even if they have no known precipitating factor. Luckily, good things can come out of the trials that God allows in our lives. Three different New Testament writers—Paul, James, and Peter—spoke of the positive attributes that come from trials.

> We can rejoice, too, when we run into problems and trials, for we know that they help us develop endurance. And endurance develops strength of character, and character strengthens our confident hope of salvation. (Roman 5:3–4 NLT)

> Consider it pure joy, my brothers and sisters, whenever you face trials of many kinds, because you know that the testing of your faith produces perseverance. (James 1:2–3)

> So be truly glad. There is wonderful joy ahead, even though you must endure many trials for a little while. These trials will show that your faith is genuine. It is being tested as fire tests and purifies gold—though your faith is far more precious than mere gold. So when your faith remains strong through many trials, it will bring you much praise and glory and honor on the day when Jesus Christ is revealed to the whole world. (1 Peter 1:6–7 NLT)

We are to rejoice in our trials due to what they produce in our lives. Trials refine us as they burn off sinful characteristics. They also build our endurance, improve our character, develop perseverance, and, most of all, increase our faith. So, even though trials may be difficult to endure, we are to take joy in knowing that godly qualities will be produced in us.

In chapter 4, we saw how the Israelites learned that God was with them in the midst of their consequences. Paul took this concept and added to it. It was during Paul's toughest trials that he saw his greatest successes in sharing the gospel, and he thrived during those times of adversity. During these harsh consequences, Paul wrote some of his greatest letters, often called the Prison Epistles of Ephesians, Philippians, Colossians, and Philemon. Those letters provide believers with some of the greatest instruction and guidance for living a holy and righteous life today.

From prison, Paul wrote, "I ask you, therefore, not to be discouraged because of my sufferings for you, which are your glory" (Ephesians 3:13). Paul knew his suffering brought out glory in Christ. I may not be in prison like Paul, but I am currently stuck at home due to the COVID-19 pandemic, along with everybody else, and am not able to conduct my usual overseas missionary travel. Spending many months in isolation has given me the time, focus, and opportunity to write this book. We all need to make the most out of the circumstances and situations we are in. Instead of complaining, ask God to show you what attributes he is trying to instill in you, and what work he wants you to complete during times of consequences and trials.

Consequences and trials have the potential to develop in us the most growth and produce the most beautiful prospects in our walk of faith. While being purified by trials, we can use these times to our advantage to change our mindset, claiming the joy of the Lord instead of being depressed and overwhelmed. We should not wallow in our own pity and be obsessive over thinking about which past events may or may not have caused our current difficulties. Instead, try to see how these trials will lead to something better than ever before, since our biggest successes come out of our biggest challenges. Embrace your trials, learn from your consequences, and get excited about the godly attributes that will develop in you.

Questions to Ponder

▶ What are some of the consequences I am still facing from past sins?

▶ When I am at my weakest, what are some strategies I can use to harness and apply the strength and power that God has given me so that I may thrive?

▶ What godly qualities have surfaced in my walk with the Lord after my toughest trials?

The Truth About Consequences

Consequences and trials can produce godly qualities in us (Paul).

Chapter II

WHAT ABOUT THOSE WHO WRONG US?

So far, we have learned about our sin and the resulting consequences, but what about everyone else? If you are like me, many people have wronged you over the years. What about those people who have hurt us or those close to us—mentally, physically, or financially—through a number of sinful practices? Will they face consequences for their sins? How will you know if they ever face judgment, and what is your role in their punishment?

In all my years of teaching, these questions have come up more than any others. To answer them, we will walk through what the Bible teaches us. We will discover how we may be treated as believers, what we should do about it, who is the judge, and how we can trust God's justice to prevail. We will also look at certain behaviors that we should be aware of, so we do not cross over into sinful territory.

Will Others Treat Us Badly?

Simply put, yes. Jesus said, "Blessed are you when people insult you, persecute you and falsely say all kinds of evil against you because of me. Rejoice and be glad, because great is your reward in heaven, for in the same way they persecuted the prophets who were before you" (Matthew 5:11–12).

Others will treat us badly for our faith. It will happen, especially when we stand strong in our mission to tell others about a loving Jesus. The good news is these verses also tell us what to do: rejoice, which can be difficult during trying times, but we should always remember the prize that awaits us in heaven. Jesus is always watching and knows what is going on.

Jesus also said, "In this world you will have trouble. But take heart! I have overcome the world" (John 16:33). What a blessing to know we, too, can overcome the world and its trouble when we follow Jesus.

Should We Take Action Against Those Who Wrong Us?

No, we should not take vengeance. As the Lord said, "'It is mine to avenge; I will repay. In due time their foot will slip; their day of disaster is near and their doom rushes upon them.' The LORD will vindicate his people" (Deuteronomy 32:35–36). The Lord alone will avenge and vindicate us, his people. This may be a very frustrating command for most of us to follow, since delivering vengeance to those who wrong us is very accepted in our society today. In addition, we tend to act impulsively when we are angry over being treated badly. However, we must let go of the anger and let God take over. God tells us he will handle it, in his way and with his timing: "Do not repay anyone evil for evil. Be careful to do what is right in the eyes of everyone. If it is possible, as far as it depends on you, live at peace with everyone. Do not take revenge, my dear friends, but leave room for God's wrath, for it is written: 'It is mine to avenge; I will repay,' says the Lord" (Romans 12:17–19).

God is concerned about justice. Many verses describe God's concern for justice for his people. Here are just three of them:

> The LORD is known by his acts of justice; the wicked are ensnared
> by the work of their hands. (Psalm 9:16)

The LORD works righteousness and justice for all the oppressed. (Psalm103:6)

And the heavens proclaim his righteousness, for he is a God of justice. (Psalm 50:6)

The apostle Paul also discussed justice in the book of 2 Thessalonians:

God is just: He will pay back trouble to those who trouble you and give relief to you who are troubled, and to us as well. This will happen when the Lord Jesus is revealed from heaven in blazing fire with his powerful angels. He will punish those who do not know God and do not obey the gospel of our Lord Jesus. They will be punished with everlasting destruction and shut out from the presence of the Lord and from the glory of his might. (2 Thessalonians 1:6–9)

So, not only is our God a God of justice, but he will provide relief for us when we face persecution. Jesus Christ will come back to earth someday to redeem all his followers, and to punish those who do not know and follow him. Jesus is the judge over all people, as he explained:

The Father judges no one. Instead, he has given the Son absolute authority to judge, so that everyone will honor the Son, just as they honor the Father. Anyone who does not honor the Son is certainly not honoring the Father who sent him. . . . Those who have done good will rise to experience eternal life, and those who have continued in evil will rise to experience judgment. I can do nothing on my own. I judge as God tells me. Therefore, my judgment is just, because I carry out the will of the one who sent me, not my own will." (John 5:22–23, 29–30 NLT)

We will all stand before Jesus Christ and face judgment, regardless of whether we are believers or not. Jesus gave us strong words to caution us against judging others. Since he alone is the judge, we have no right to judge others. If we judge others harshly, we, too, will be held to that same standard. Jesus said, "Do not judge others, and you will not be judged. For you will be treated as you treat others. The standard you use in judging is the standard by which you will be judged" (Matthew 7:1–2 NLT).

Jesus also gave us the perfect example in John 8, with the story of the woman caught in adultery. When, as a trap, the Pharisees brought her to Jesus for judgment, Jesus highlighted their own sinful judgmental behavior: "Let any one of you who is without sin be the first to throw a stone at her" (John 8:7). Consequently, they all turned and walked away. We should not be "throwing stones" at others.

The same rules apply for forgiveness. We cannot expect to be forgiven if we do not forgive others. Jesus said, "For if you forgive other people when they sin against you, your heavenly Father will also forgive you. But if you do not forgive others their sins, your Father will not forgive your sins" (Matthew 6:14–15).

I love how the Bible never lets us get away with anything. We are also not to harbor bitterness or hold a grudge against another. Bitterness comes when we hold on to anger or disappointment when we are treated badly and allow it to consume us. Holding a grudge means not completely forgiving someone and continuing to treat them badly.

> Watch out that no poisonous root of bitterness grows up to trouble you, corrupting many. (Hebrews 12:15 NLT)

> Do not seek revenge or bear a grudge against anyone among your people, but love your neighbor as yourself. I am the LORD. (Leviticus 19:18)

> Do not gloat when your enemy falls; when they stumble, do not

let your heart rejoice, or the LORD will see and disapprove and turn his wrath away from them. (Proverbs 24:17–18)

How Does This Relate to Me Today?

We all live in a tough world today. Was there ever a time when people were always nice to each other, or does that only exist on TV shows like *Leave It to Beaver*? Regardless, the Bible gives us clear guidance on how to behave when we are wronged by others. These may be hard lessons for all of us, as the Bible verses above go against accepted practices in today's sinful world. We live in a world where everyone has ideas and opinions about what is right and wrong, and most of those opinions are not based in biblical truths.

Sadly, it has always been common for humans to be cruel to each other, and these days there are even more ways to insult, degrade, and unleash anger on others than in the past, primarily through the internet and social media. We need to learn not to be offended by every negative comment that comes our way, but to release them to God and let it go. We need to accept that there will always be people who just do not like us. In all my years in the military, I learned no matter how hard I tried, some people just did not like me, no matter how kind and generous I tried to be toward them.

As I was working on this chapter, a young woman whom I mentor called to ask for some advice about a difficult situation she was having with a coworker who was treating her poorly. As she explained her story, I was able to recount several similar work situations concerning a difficult or untrustworthy colleague. I am sure many of you can relate to having difficulties with work colleagues and unfair work situations, as it is very common in the diverse environment we work in today. Thankfully, together we discussed ways she could act in a godly and righteous manner to her coworker, primarily by avoiding my past mistakes.

I can remember times when I have been treated poorly by just about everyone. At times, it was a reaction to my faith; sometimes it was a response to one of my choices or actions that impacted them in a negative way; and occasionally it was purely a personality conflict. One time I received a very hurtful and unsolicited email from an individual I thought was a good friend and fellow believer. When I prayed about it, the Lord told me that the enemy was using him to steal my joy and to try to discourage me in my walk with Jesus. Sometimes we need to see these hurtful events in our lives as attacks from the enemy and not from the people who matter to us. I am now very careful to make sure the enemy does not use me to attack or steal the joy in someone else's life.

How we react when we are treated badly is important. Regardless of how we are treated, we are told by Jesus to love everyone. The good news is we do not have to do that alone; we can ask Jesus to help us love others. When I have a difficult time loving someone, I ask the Lord to show me that individual through his eyes. The Lord created every human being and loves them all, so I try to see people how God created them and with the love he has for them.

We also need to look at our actions to make sure we are not offending others without realizing it. When someone treats you badly, ask them if you did something that hurt or offended them, and apologize. Check your own actions to ensure you treated them in the same manner you like to be treated. Have you put yourself in their shoes to look at the issues from their perspective? Oftentimes when we do that, we will get a clearer picture of what the true issue is and how to best resolve the situation together in love.

Many expect to see justice prevail on their watch, but that does not always happen. There are many people out there who have wronged me, lied about me, and damaged me personally and professionally. For most of these people, I have not seen them suffer any consequences, and I may never see it. Those actions may not happen until they stand before Jesus Christ. Whenever it does happen, it will be between them and the Lord, and I only need to know God will judge them as it is written in his Word. I try to remember I never really know what is going on in their lives, what hurts or pain they have experienced, or what events in their background led to their behavior or actions against me. My job is just to forgive them, bless them, pray they see the error of their ways, and turn the situation over to God.

However, I have also seen people who have wronged me suffer consequences. An individual whom I was once very close with changed in his feelings toward me. In his anger against me, he took actions to jeopardize my military career. He said many damaging and untrue things to work associates and some mutual friends, and he even had a few people write false statements against me. He made claims that could have resulted in the loss of my government security clearance. He was not successful in any attempts to damage my career, and I knew the Lord was protecting me. However, over the course of the next several years, due to his own actions, he lost his military career and his security clearance, which was very damaging to his financial status. I believe he suffered consequences for targeting my career, and possibly others' careers as well. Over the course of several years, I had to forgive him over and over again for continued actions he took against me. One of the main Bible verses I used was: "On the contrary: 'If your enemy is hungry, feed him; if he is thirsty, give him something to drink. In doing this, you will heap burning coals on his head.' Do not be overcome by evil, but overcome evil with good" (Romans 12:20–21).

As hard as it was, whenever I saw him, I did my best to bless him, as the Bible tells us to "bless those who persecute you; bless and do not curse" (Romans 12:14). Now, I must admit, the thought of him having burning coals heaped on his head gave me some feeling of justice. When I started taking pleasure in this thought, however, I had to check myself and remember not to judge his actions or wish any harm upon him, no matter how intentionally harmful his actions seemed toward me. I had to go to the Lord and ask for help in forgiving him many times. Toward the end, I began to feel sorry for him.

Tragically, sinful behaviors run rampant in today's society. As believers, we need to stand above these mannerisms and quickly repent when we fall prey to them.

Most people who have an issue with the Christian church had a bad experience with someone who claimed to be a believer, then judged them and treated them in an ungodly manner. It is terrible when believers judge other believers just because they sin in a different manner.[10] So many Christians are hypocrites. Some of the individuals who have hurt me the most have been people who proclaimed to be followers of Jesus. Some were self-righteous and judged me on standards they did not follow themselves. Others were professing believers who lived secret lives of sin and became angry at me when I confronted them about their behaviors. We need to live and walk out our faith daily and remember our actions speak louder than our words.

Do you still hold unforgiveness in your heart against someone? I often hear the phrase, "I will forgive them, but I will never forget what they did to me." Honestly, that is not true forgiveness. Since God forgets our sins, we need to forget the sins of others. I have a close family member who has been holding a grudge against me for many years, and no matter how many times I have reached out, apologized, and tried anything to rebuild that relationship, all my attempts have been futile. I know firsthand how exhausting it can be emotionally, mentally, and physically to hold onto such a strong grudge for so long. I pray he will turn it over to God and be released from it. I believe this is a common way that Satan keeps believers in discord, as it can stop their maturity and intimacy with the Lord.

I, too, have sinned in these areas. I used to hold grudges for a really long time. However, I realized that it cost me a lot of wasted energy and self-peace. I learned it was better to give them over to God. Early in my military career, I was very judgmental against a woman my coworker was dating. She had already been divorced twice due to two unfaithful husbands. I was very quick to criticize her to my coworker, proclaiming she must have been a terrible wife to have two husbands cheat on her. Well, within the next eleven years, I also became a twice-divorced woman from unfaithful husbands. Ouch!

It is good to seek the Lord often to ask him if you are holding onto any unforgiveness, bitterness, grudges, or sinful habits in your life.

Continue to examine yourself, confess, and repent when you slip into these behaviors.

The Bible teaches us how to feel about those who wrong us and those we consider our enemies. Jesus said,

> You have heard the law that says, "Love your neighbor" and hate your enemy. But I say, love your enemies! Pray for those who persecute you! In that way, you will be acting as true children of your Father in heaven. For he gives his sunlight to both the evil and the good, and he sends rain on the just and the unjust alike. If you love only those who love you, what reward is there for that? Even corrupt tax collectors do that much. If you are kind only to your friends, how are you different from anyone else? Even pagans do that. But you are to be perfect, even as your Father in heaven is perfect. (Matt. 5:43–48 NLT)

Do you love only your family and friends, or are you willing to extend God's love to all those who treat you poorly? Nowadays, when someone wrongs me, I immediately feel sorry for them. I do not get angry (well, at least I do not stay angry). Why? They are messing with a child of the Most High God, as I am God's beloved daughter and I am coheir with Jesus Christ in the kingdom of God. So when someone is messing with me, they are really messing with God, and they will suffer the consequences according to his Word. I do not need to do a thing, other than show them God's love and forgive them in my heart. I know I really love someone and have forgiven them when I grieve for the consequences they will receive for their sins. It is important you do not relieve your own anger by wishing harm on those who wrong you via God's wrath. Instead, try to release your anger by thinking how bad things must be in their lives that they feel the need to act so badly against you.

If you find yourself acting out with these destructive behaviors, it is time for a personal assessment or professional help. The idea is to take a step back when you have a strong emotion and to analyze *why* you were triggered and what sorts of distorted thoughts your brain automatically jumped to concerning these people. Then restructure and rationalize those thoughts, realizing they are not true or helpful and may lead you to harmful behaviors and thoughts.

I am not advocating we let people take advantage of us or idly sit by when we are wronged, but I believe, with God by our side, he will guide our actions in the right direction. Twice, I have been injured and treated badly and decided to take companies to small claims court. They would not admit and accept their faults or take concrete actions to ensure others would not be harmed, and that upset me. Both times, after much prayer, I felt the Holy Spirit guide my steps. I persisted because it was important that others would not have to suffer the way that I did, even if it meant I had to spend more money and time fighting for what was right. Sometimes we do need to take action on something that is unjust, but doing it in a respectful and lawful way is how to make a change in the world, rather than just seeking out our own personal revenge.

How glorious it is to know that our God is righteous and just. We just need to trust in him and his timing. I love this quote from Billy Graham: "It is the Holy Spirit's job to convict, God's job to judge, and my job to love." So trust God, and pray for and release those who have wronged you to God.

Questions to Ponder

▶ Do I truly believe God is a just God? If I don't, how can I prove it to myself?

▶ Who is someone I still feel angry at for a past action, and what can I do to finally move on?

▶ Do I pray and grieve for those who wrong me? The next time somebody wrongs me, will I look at them through God's eyes?

The Truth About Consequences
God is just, and all will face consequences.

Chapter 12

IT'S UP TO YOU

started this book by daring you to accept the truths laid out in the Bible concerning sin and consequences. Now that you have finished, you should realize that only you have the power to make changes in your own life. The great news is you have the ability to do it with Jesus by your side. Call on the name of Jesus Christ to help you. I think the most powerful prayer we can ever say is just to cry out "Jesus!" He knows what is going on, and he just wants you to surrender the problem or situation to him.

We have seen how different sins can lead to different consequences, ranging from generational to immediate. I hope it helped you to become a little more self-aware of your past sins and the consequences that came from them, in addition to your current thoughts, actions, and strength within—and I hope it helped you to feel confident in finding God's truths in the Bible on your own.

My primary goal for this book is for you to understand the truth about your sin and the consequences you will face. Realizing there will be consequences as well as forgiveness should temper your sinful actions significantly. I hope this book leads you to a much deeper level in your own spiritual life, with several ideas about how to continuously improve your relationship and intimacy with our loving Father God. I pray that those of you who did not have a relationship with Jesus Christ now understand him to be your Savior and see how important it is to follow him daily.

The Lord has a good plan for your life. When we learn to hear the voice of the Holy Spirit and allow it to guide us, we will be following God's path for us. If and when we sin, we should know and understand the consequences we will face. That does not mean our lives will suddenly be easier, but we have the confidence of knowing, whatever we are going through, we are not going through it alone. The Lord will always be with us, helping us and guiding us through the trials and consequences we will face in this sinful world.

Just like the apostle Paul wrote to the church at Thessalonica, this is my prayer for you:

> So we keep on praying for you, asking our God to enable you to live a life worthy of his call. May he give you the power to accomplish all the good things your faith prompts you to do. Then the name of our Lord Jesus will be honored because of the way you live, and you will be honored along with him. This is all made possible because of the grace of our God and Lord, Jesus Christ. (2 Thessalonians 1:11–12 NLT)

The last page in this book is for you. I want you to tear it out and put it somewhere you will see often, like in your Bible, on your refrigerator, or taped to your bathroom mirror. It lists the ten key points in the book. Let it remind you daily how to keep focus on the truth about consequences.

Just like I dared you in the introduction to take a hard look at yourself, your spiritual life, and your actions, I now dare you to go out into the world and live out the truths I have presented to you. Do not forget how much the Lord loves you and that he is with you every step of your walk. This should give you joy regardless of what you face. So, go forth in your walk of faith, being obedient to the Word, and trusting the Lord is with you in every circumstance and consequence.

Heavenly Father, thank you this book has been your vessel to touch the lives and spirits of everyone who has read it. Let your Word continue to convict, and let my words remind the readers of your will and your ways. In Jesus Christ's holy name, amen.

THE TRUTH ABOUT CONSEQUENCES

1. Sin can result in generational consequences (Adam and Eve).

2. One careless sin can lead to lifelong consequences (Moses and Aaron).

3. The Lord provides for us in the midst of our consequences (the Israelites in the desert).

4. Expect rewards for faithful service to God (Caleb and Joshua).

5. As our sins multiply, so do the consequences (David).

6. We can't run from God; he always finds us (Jonah).

7. True repentance can turn destruction into everlasting life (Nineveh's Redemption).

8. God knows your true motives, so continually strive for righteousness because consequences can be immediate (Ananias and Sapphira).

9. Consequences and trials can produce godly qualities in us (Paul).

10. God is just, and all will face consequences.

·

Notes

1. Grant Osborne, gen ed., Life Application Bible Commentary, John (Carol Stream, IL: Tyndale, 1993), 86.

2. Earl D. Radmacher, gen. ed., *The Nelson Study Bible, NKJV* (Nashville: Thomas Nelson, 1997), 2,140.

3. Rose Eveleth, "Could a Whale Accidentally Swallow You? It Is Possible" Smithsonianmag.com, February 25, 2013.

4. E. B. Pusey (Barnes' Notes), *The Minor Prophets, A Commentary* (Grand Rapids, MI: Baker Books, 1961, 1996), 415.

5. Grant Osborne, gen. ed., Life Application Bible Commentary, Acts (Carol Stream, IL: Tyndale, 1999), 74.

6 . Warren Wiersbe, The Bible Exposition Commentary, New Testament Vol 1 (Colorado Springs, CO: David C. Cook, 1989), 421.

7 . Matthew Boffey, "5 Insights for Interpreting the Deaths of Ananias and Sapphira," Logos Talk, May 1, 2019, https://blog.logos.com/author/matthewboffey/.

8. Jack W. Hayford, gen ed, *Spirit-Filled Life Bible* (Nashville: Thomas Nelson, 1991), 1,633.

9 . Philip Wijaya, "What Is Righteousness?" Christianity.com, December 16, 2019.

10. David Bartlett, "Don't Judge Others Because They Sin Differently Than You Do," *Christian Living*, November 19, 2015, https://davidmbartlett.wordpress.com/2015/11/19/don't-judge-others-because-they-sin-differently-than-you-do/.

ABOUT THE AUTHOR

 Merrily Madero is called to preach, teach, and serve around the world. She is an ordained minister with Assemblies of God through the Michigan District, but splits her time between Saint Helen, Michigan and Colorado Springs, Colorado. Merrily is founder and president of Merrily Madero Ministries, M3 International, which focuses on preaching the Word of God, biblical teaching for several Bible schools, along with leadership training and development for churches, secular universities, hospitals and other nonprofit organizations. Merrily's practical leadership experience comes from serving in the US Air Force for thirty years, retiring as a Colonel after commanding four large organizations. Merrily has Bachelor's degrees in both Theology and Mechanical Engineering, and three advanced degrees from Troy University, National Defense University, and Air Command and Staff College.

To contact Merrily for preaching, speaking, or training, write her at:

MerrilyMadero@gmail.com

Or

M3 International
P.O. Box 76322
Colorado Springs, CO 80970-6322

Be sure to check out her Website at: www.M3international.org